Hokum:

Theory and Scales for Fiddle Tunes and Fiddle Improvisation

by Leon Grizzard

2 3 4 5 6 7 8 9 0

COPYRIGHT © 1997 BY LEON GRIZZARD.
EXCLUSIVE SALES AGENT: MEL BAY PUBLICATIONS, INC., PACIFIC, MO 63069.
ALL RIGHTS RESERVED. INTERNATIONAL COPYRIGHT SECURED. B.M.I. MADE AND PRINTED IN U.S.A.
No part of this publication may be reproduced in whole or in part, or stored in a retrieval system, or transmitted in any form
or by any means, electronic, mechanical, photocopy, recording, or otherwise, without written permission of the publisher.

Visit us on the Web at http://www.melbay.com — E-mail us at email@melbay.com

Table of Contents

Introduction 5

Basics 7

D Major 10

G Major 18

A Major 28

C Major 36

F Major 44

E Major 46

Dominants 48

A Dominant 49

D Dominant 55

G Dominant 58

C Dominant 61

E Dominant 63

B Dominant 66

Extended and Altered Dominants 68

IV Chord - Lydian 70

Mixolydian 71

A Minor 76

E Minor 90

D Minor 99

Diminished 105

Blues 112

A Modest Essay 118

Postscript 120

Introduction

This book is written for three main purposes: (1) to teach music theory and scales as applied to fiddle tunes in the American/Celtic traditions; (2) to teach fiddle improvisation; and (3) to present additional material to help the fiddler who wants to play in other popular styles.

This is not a lick book, nor is it a book of transcriptions of great fiddle solos for you to study and emulate. This book will teach you the theoretical framework of fiddle tunes and of fiddle soloing; the scales and arpeggios that fiddlers actually use, whether they know it or not. If you improvise or play variations on tunes now, you are already using these scales and arpeggios, and I hope the book can help you understand this language you speak by ear, and help you understand what works and why.

Major Scale Tune Approach

We will look at major sounds in general: the basic three note major chord; the major pentatonic scale; and the major scale. We will see how those three expressions of the major sound are found in fiddle tunes. We will have exercises to get you playing the various chord arpeggios and scales from memory, and in combination with each other.

For improvisation, the basic approach is to change scales with every chord change. When playing over a C chord, you play some sort of C scale; when playing over an F chord, you play some sort of F scale; and when you play over a G7 chord you play a G dominant scale. This is not as complicated or as much to learn as it might seem at first. A handful of arpeggios and scales will cover most tunes in the important fiddle keys, D, G, A, and C.

In addition to this chord scale approach, you will improvise by just playing melodically in the key you are in (i.e., when playing *Liberty* in D you will noodle around with the D major scale, on all the chord changes). But even then, it is important to play the right notes from the D major scale. For example, if you play over a D chord, in the key of D, and try to play just using the notes G, C♯, B and E, it just won't sound as harmonious as using the notes of the D chord, D, F♯, and A, prominently in your phrase. Makes sense. Often, I will tell you to play chord based scales, changing scales with each chord change, and you will still be playing all notes from the key you are in; it's a matter of note selection.

Of course, the chord changes to fiddle tunes are not engraved in stone; there are variants, and there may some ambiguity about which is the right or best chord. However, with major scale tunes, the basic harmony will usually be clearly suggested by the music, even though the chord progression could always be gussied up. You will be thoroughly versed in fiddle tune chords, and be in a position to make intelligent choices about the chord changes and what scales to use.

Modal Tune Approach

For tunes written in the modes, mixolydian, aeolian, and dorian, the chord scale approach is not satisfactory. Modern harmony does not fit modal tunes very well, and the chords are not so clearly suggested by the music as in major scale tunes. Some traditionalists say these tunes should have only very simple, "neo-modal" accompaniment, meaning drones or simpler structures than our modern three note chords. Therefore, with modal tunes, the emphasis will be on learning the scales, and improvising melodically, although we will look at the chords generally used. There will be a chapter on the mixolydian mode by itself, and we will look at the dorian and aeolian modes in chapters dealing with minor sounds in general: the minor chord arpeggio; the minor pentatonic scale; and the two minor modes, dorian and aeolian. We will also look at minor chords as they occur in modern popular music.

Bowings, etc.

Whatever. This is a theory book that teaches scales, and not a real scale exercise book, such as Whistler's *Scales in First Position for Violin*. The examples are intended to be generic sounding, and are generally written in all eighth notes, with little syncopation. The emphasis is on teaching scales on the fiddle, but not on how to play them in tune, with different bowings, etc. My intent is that you play the exercises in whatever style you comfortable, taking as many or as few notes per bow as you want, and playing with as little or as much swing as you like.

Do it Yourself

After each little section of the book, I will say "try that on your own," or words to that effect. Those are the most important words in the book; studying this stuff will only help you if you play it by ear, and put it to use in tunes you now play. When I work through music books, and there are a bunch of tasks set out at the end of the chapter, and they are not all written out, I usually skip 'em. I expect more of you.

The Dark Side of Scale Theory

If you depend on just running scales and arpeggios in your playing, you will sound machinelike, and unmelodic. When learning scales and arpeggios, there is a period when you have to play them mechanically, to get them under your fingers. You have to get beyond that. There are too many little Pagginoodles running around already. The study of scales is a means to an end. The purpose of the study is to put sounds under your fingertips, so that when you think a musical thought in a given harmonic context, you will know how to produce that thought, with confidence and accuracy.

Basics

Most of the theory is spread out in the course of the book. To start, you need to know the basic concepts of music spelling and counting. Many of you know this stuff already, but I ask you to read through it to review, and to make sure you really have it.

Western music divides the octave (the distance from one tone to the tone double its frequency) into twelve equal intervals, each of which is called a half step. This corresponds to the distance between any two adjacent keys on the piano, or any consecutive frets on a guitar. Two half steps are called a whole step. Most scales, including the major, minor, and modal scales, use seven of these twelve half steps. (We will also study the five note pentatonic scale, and the diminished scale, which uses eight notes.)

I know all of you know this, but: we use the letters of the alphabet A through G, plus the symbols ♭ (lower a pitch by a half step), and ♯ (raise a pitch by a half step), to name the twelve half steps. The twelve half steps are named, from C to C:

C; C♯/D♭; D; D♯/E♭; E; F; F♯/G♭; G; G♯/A♭; A; A♯/B♭; B.

(C♯ and D♭ are, of course, the same pitch, just described in terms of its relationship to C and D, respectively.)

We use numbers to describe the interval, or distance between two notes. Starting from the lower note, from some kind of C (C, C♯, or C♭) to some kind of E (E, E♯, or E♭), is described as being an interval of a third. C=1, D=2, E=3, get it? Similarly, from some kind of C to some kind of A, is an interval of a sixth: C=1, D=2, E=3, F=4, G=5, A=6. This needs to be refined a little bit, since C to E is 5 half steps, whereas C to E♭ is only four half steps. We use the terms major, minor, perfect, augmented and diminished to described the intervals more specifically. For reference, here are the most common intervals:

INTERVAL	DISTANCE	EXAMPLE
minor second	1 half step	C to D♭
major second	2 half steps	C to D
minor third	3 half steps	C to E♭
major third	4 half steps	C to E
perfect fourth	5 half steps	C to F

augmented fourth diminished fifth	6 half steps 6 half steps	C to F♯ C to G♭
perfect fifth	7 half steps	C to G
minor sixth	8 half steps	C to A♭
major sixth	9 half steps	C to A
minor seventh	10 half steps	C to B♭
major seventh	11 half steps	C to B
octave	12 half steps	C to c

Generally, intervals of a 4th and 5th have three possible qualities: perfect, diminished, and augmented; while intervals of a 2nd, 3rd, 6th, and 7th, have two possible qualities: major and minor (there are other qualities of these intervals but they are rare; we will see an augmented 2nd later in the book).

Scales

A scale is a set of notes used to play tunes. The major scale is the most common scale used in Western music. A scale, such as the major scale, can be described with a formula, or the sequence of whole and half steps needed to produce the particular scale. For example, the major scale is spelled, from its root: whole step; whole step; half step; whole step; whole step; whole step; half step. A look at the piano keyboard, where the C major scale lies on all white keys, will show this is true. And no matter what note you start on, be it C, of E♭, if you follow that same sequence of whole and half steps, you will produce a major scale.

Scale Degrees

The different notes of scales are often described by number. For example, in the key D, D is called 1, because it is the first note of the D major scale; E is called 2, because it is the second note, and so on. They are also called scale degrees (i.e. E is the second scale degree in the key of D major). For scale spelling, the major scale is the usual scale of reference. For example, the major scale is spelled 1, 2, 3, 4, 5, 6, 7. Other scales are spelled according to what alterations have to be made to the major scale (i.e. the natural minor scale is spelled 1, 2, ♭3, 4, 5, ♭6, ♭7, indicating that scale degrees 1, 2, 4, and 5 are the same as the major scale, but scale degrees 3, 6, and 7 have to be lowered by one half step from their major scale spellings).

Chords

Western music uses chords to harmonize, or accompany, music. A chord is three or more notes played at the same time. The basic chords are formed from a scale, as follows: play a note, skip the next note, play the note after that, skip the next note, and play the note after that. In other words, every other note (ascending), for a total for three notes. Chords can be constructed on any scale degree, and that is how we get the basic chords for a given key or scale. These basic three note chords are called **triads**. The notes in a triad are called the root, 3rd and 5th; start on the root, skip 2, play 3, skip 4, play 5.

Chords, like scales, can be described with formulae. Like scales, these formulae use the major scale as a reference. For example, a major chord is spelled 1, 3, 5, meaning the first, third and fifth notes of a major scale starting on the root of the chord (every other note, for a total of three notes, right?). The C major chord is spelled C, E, G, which are the first, third, and fifth notes of the C major scale. The D major chord is spelled D, F♯, A, which are the first, third, and fifth notes of the D major scale. Minor chords are spelled 1, ♭3, 5, meaning that the first and fifth notes of the major scale are used, but for the 3rd of the chord, the third note of the major scale must be lowered by a half step. The C minor chord is spelled C, E♭, G, while the C major chord is spelled C, E, G.

Chord Symbols

Upper and lower case Roman numerals are often used to indicate both the scale degree on which the chord is built, and the basic chord type, with capital Roman numerals for major chords, and lower case Roman numerals for minor chords. For example, I, IV and V indicate major chords built on the 1st, 4th and 5th scale degrees, while ii, iii, and vi indicate minor chords built on the 2nd, 3rd and 6th scale degrees. You will also see M and Maj for major chords, and m and min for minor chords.

Both chords and scales use similar terminology; you should be able to tell from the context whether someone is talking about a note being the 3rd scale degree of a scale, or the 3rd of a chord.

The Major Scale

Since about 1650-1700 CE, Western music has been based on the major scale, and almost all popular music of today is written in the major scale (some music uses the minor scale, regarded as an honored but a lesser relative). The last few decades have seen a renewed interest in other scales in jazz, Celtic based music, and in rock, but there haven't been any Top Forty hits in mixolydian. Most fiddle tunes, in both American and Celtic styles are in the major scale, so we will start our studies there. We will look at three major type elements: the major triad; the major pentatonic scale; and the major scale.

I, IV, & V Chords

For the first of about a hundred times: **there are three major triads in the major scale, whose roots are on the first, fourth and fifth scale degrees; referred to as I, IV, and V.** These are the most important chords in the major scale. Most fiddle tunes use only these three chords; many use only I and V.

D Major

This first chapter deals with D major sounds, all notated in the key of D major.

We will start with the basic D major triad (three note chord), which is spelled: D, F#, A.

Then we will look at the D major pentatonic scale: D, E, F#, A, B.

Finally, we will look at the D major scale itself: D, E, F#, G, A, B, C# (note that if we start on the note D, and construct a major scale, we have to play F# and C# rather than F and C; this is reflected in the key signature).

D Major Triad

What you need to do is memorize the D major triad, and all the other scales and arpeggios in the book. You should be able to rattle off a major triad starting on any note. Arpeggios are not just some pedagogical exercise. They can make an elegant pickup:

And look at the first full measure of each these excerpts:

Soldier's Joy

Cincinnati Hornpipe

Liverpool Hornpipe

O'Conner's Favorite

Mississippi Sawyer

Some tunes are basically triads with connecting notes:

Hell Among the Yearlings

Triad arpeggios are an important building block of melodies. Consider that a D chord may appear in a bunch of different keys of modes, for example: D major, G major, A major, E dorian and A dorian. The D triad arpeggio fits any of those occurrences, it being the chord itself. So it is worthwhile to know the D triad its ownself, apart from its appearance in the key of D major.

The same is true of our next subject.

The Major Pentatonic Scale

The major pentatonic scale is one of the most important scales in American/Celtic traditional music. **It is also the usual major scale type for rock music,** rather than the actual major scale (Allman Brothers to Aerosmith, learn this and the minor pentatonic for blues playing, and you are ready to mainstream rock). Pentatonic means five notes, and that is just what the major pentatonic scale is: five notes corresponding to the 1st, 2nd, 3rd, 5th, and 6th scale degrees of the major scale. It is sometimes referred to as the 6/9 scale, because it starts with the basic major triad, 1, 3, 5, and adds to it the 6th and 9th (same as 2nd) scale degrees.

Although its notes correspond to 1, 2, 3, 5, 6 of the major scale, the major pentatonic scale is not exactly a subset of the major scale. It is a very old and very widespread scale found in the music of (almost?) all the peoples of Europe, and is found in folk and tribal music from Asia, Africa and the Americas. Many parts of fiddle tunes are completely or almost completely major pentatonic. It has all whole steps and minor thirds (no half steps), so it proceeds by nice big steps, giving it an open sound.

Although the pentatonic scale is not exactly part of the major scale, it is helpful to compare the two scales. We know that the major scale has seven notes, and the pentatonic is the same as five of them. What is left out? The 4th scale degree and 7th scale degree are not present in the major pentatonic scale.

When played over the I chord (like D major pentatonic played over the D chord in the key of D major), the absence of the 4th and 7th scale degrees contributes to the harmonious, pleasing sound of the pentatonic scale. The 4th scale degree is only a half step above the 3rd of the chord, and this is considered discordant. The 7th scale degree is only a half step below the root of the chord (an octave higher), and, much like the 4th scale degree, is thought to clash.

The major pentatonic scale can be played over any major type chord of he same root, including major chords, major and dominant 7th chords, and 6th chords. And so, like the triad, it is useful to learn the pentatonic scale from various root tones, to be able to play, for example, the D major pentatonic scale over any D major based chord, in whatever key it may appear.

We will begin, then, with the D major pentatonic scale, spelled: D, E, F♯, A, B.

D Major Pentatonic Scale

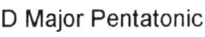

Here is a diagram of the D major pentatonic scale: D, E, F♯, A, B. The diagram on the left shows the scale in one octave, and the diagram on the right shows it extended up and down a few notes.

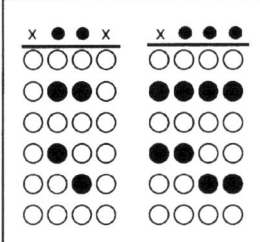

We now have "Write Your Own Hornpipe Time." We start with a D major triad:

Here is the same arpeggio, alternating with measures of D major pentatonic. A few examples start you off; then a blank measure appears after the arpeggio. Put in your own D major pentatonic runs. Just start a run on any of five notes of the D major pentatonic scale. You'll figure it out.

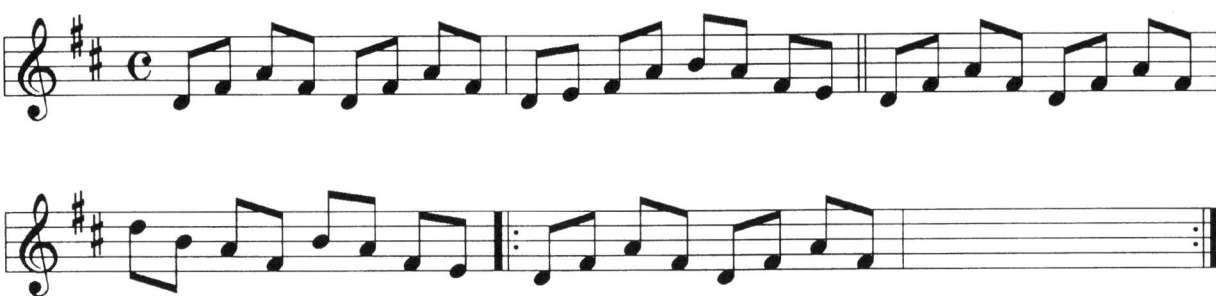

Here is *Oh, Susannah* again. The third measure is blank. Fill it with the D major pentatonic scale.

Oh, Susannah

Don't worry about trying to tie your improvised line to the original melody; just play the D major pentatonic scale, starting on different notes. Soon you will able to use scales for controlled improvisation. Until then, just play hokum. The way to incorporate new scales or licks in your playing is to get them out there and working. Just cram them in, and eventually you will make the little adjustments which make them fit, and make them a part of your personal style. Try the D major pentatonic scale over some D chord measures in a tune or two in your repertoire, in any key you find those D chords.

D Major Scale

The D major scale is spelled D, E, F♯, G, A, B, C♯. The major scale adds the 4th and 7th scale degrees, G and C♯ in D major, to the major pentatonic scale.

Unlike the major triad and major pentatonic scale, the major scale is only used in its home key. That is, the D major triad and D major pentatonic scale can be used over any D major chord, in any key, while the D major scale can only be used in the key of D major (in traditional music).

Not to dwell on minutae, but: when playing over the I chord, the 4th scale degree is the least used note. The 7th scale degree is the next least used note. All that means, on a practical level, is know both the major pentatonic scale and the major scale; you may often find your musical thoughts, and many parts of fiddle tunes, are pentatonic.

Here are some repertoire excerpts, using the D major scale, or at least including G or C♯:

D Major Scale

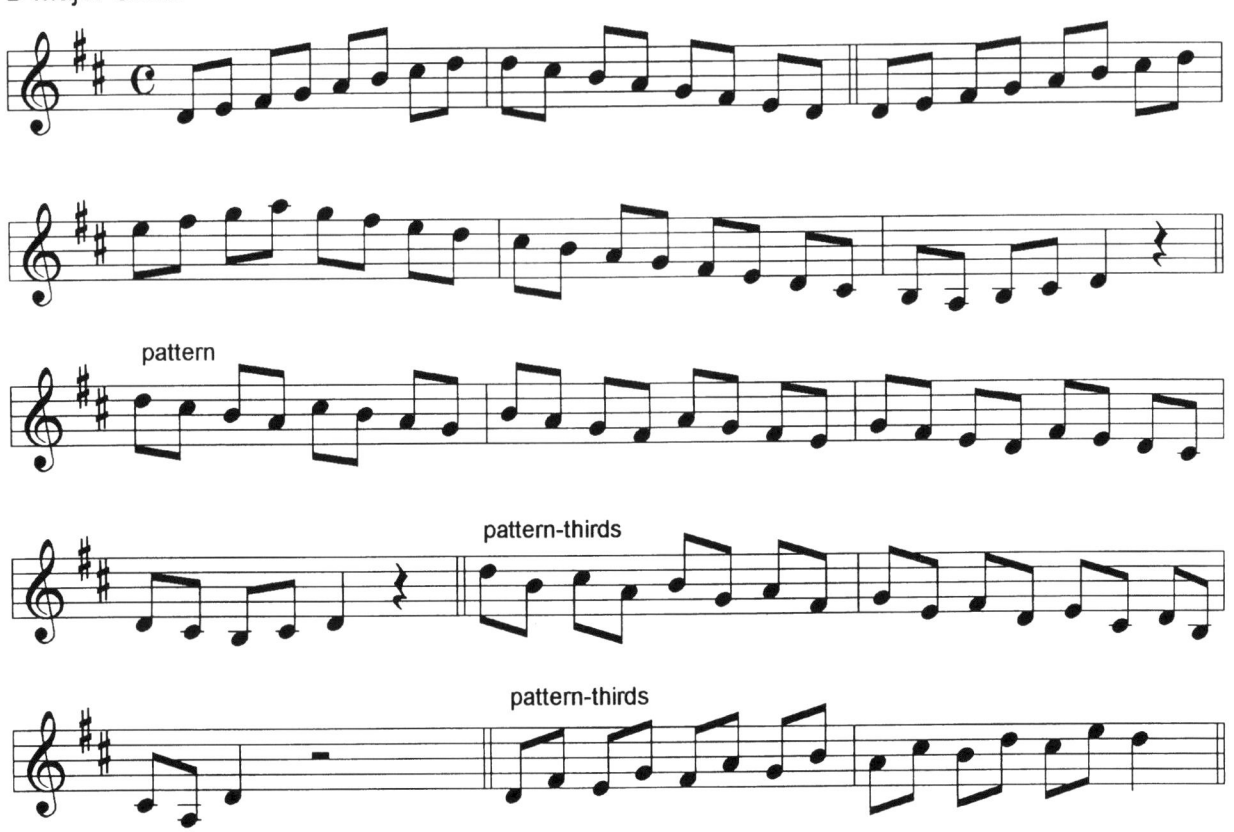

Here are the triad arpeggios built on each scale degree of the D major scale:

Here are the seventh chord arpeggios in the key of D major. That means we have kept on with our every-other-note method of chord building, and are spelling chords 1, 3, 5, 7.

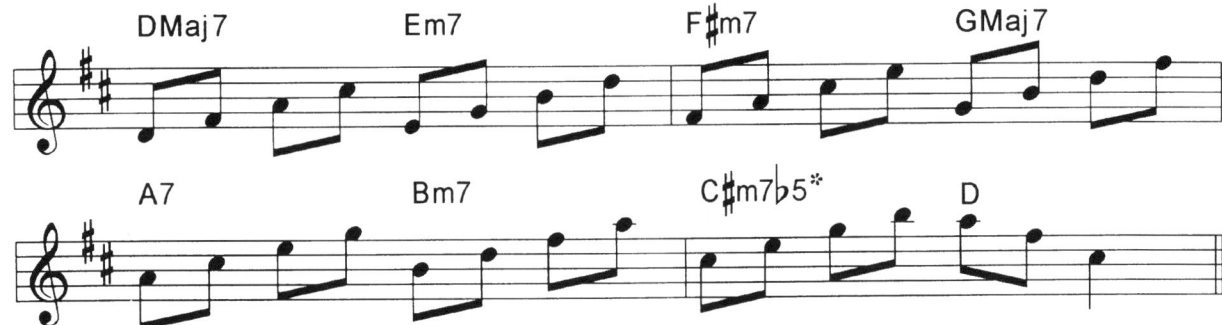

*This chord is properly called a half diminished seventh chord, but is commonly called a minor seventh flat fifth chord.

As with the D major pentatonic scale, you now need to memorize and play the D major scale by ear. If you need the structure, go back to our "Write Your Own Hornpipe" exercise, using major scale runs rather than major pentatonic runs. Stick some D major scale runs in some fiddle tunes in D.

We will conclude our D major studies by looking at a non-traditional use of the major scale. You dedicated Old Timers can skip this section.

The Major Seventh Sound

Earlier in this chapter, I told you the seventh scale degree of the major scale, (C♯ in the key of D major), was considered to be somewhat discordant over the I chord, and so was not usually emphasized, but used off the beat, as a passing note between the 1st and 6th scale degree, or used to decorate the 1st scale degree. We now embrace the major seventh.

Beginning in the early 1950's, the major seventh chord became the usual I and IV chord of the popular song segment of the jazz repertoire (ballads, Tin Pan Alley and show tunes, etc). If you use our play-every-other-note method of chord building, and build 1, 3, 5, 7 on either the 1st or 4th scale degrees of the major scale, you get a major seventh chord, a major triad with an 11 half step major seventh on top. It has a kind of sweet dissonance. Before that, the 6th scale degree was the most common addition to the major triad to give some color to I and IV.

Similarly, the sweet dissonance of the major seventh scale degree has become a basic jazz melody sound, and has become accepted in a wide range of popular music. It is your basic schmaltz sound, for boozy, sentimental country, insipid pop love songs, etc. Really, it's a good sound to know, but you can overdo it. Here are a couple of runs emphasizing the 7th scale degree, C♯ in the key of D:

If you can get a guitarist to work with you a little, here is a jazz vamp which will substitute for two measures of D or DMaj7. Play around with the D major scale, giving some emphasis to the 7th scale degree, C♯. You're Stephane Grappelli, in first position. The guitarist should play DMaj7 for a jazz sound, or D for a more country swing sound.

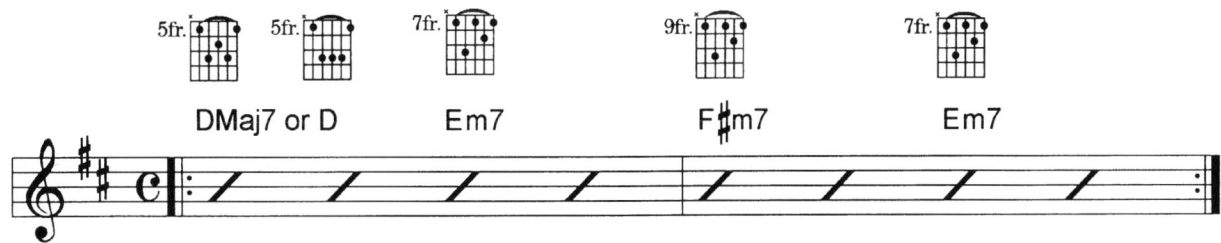

G Major

Now we start into G major sounds.

We will start with the G major triad: G, B, D;

Then we will look at the G major pentatonic scale: G, A, B, D, E;

Finally, the G major scale: G, A, B, C, D, E, F♯.

Actually, what we will do is pause after the G major pentatonic scale, and combine the G pentatonic and D pentatonic scales, for a little harmonic variety.

G Major Triad

Now, of course, you need to memorize the G major triad; how to play it, what the notes are, and where they fall on the fingerboard.

Look for our G triad, G, B, D, in the first full measure of each of these excerpts:

Irish Washerwoman

You are now sophisticated enough to recognize that the note C in the last measure is simply connecting two chord tones, D and B.

Golden Eagle Hornpipe

Mississippi Hornpipe

Delaware Hornpipe

Key-West Hornpipe

The Boys from Scart

G Major Pentatonic

Now the G major pentatonic scale: G, A, B, D, E.

G Major
Pentatonic

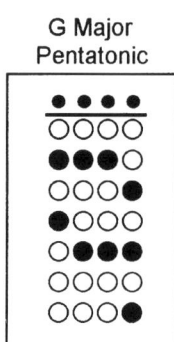

Here is a diagram of the G major pentatonic scale, shown over two octaves, plus A and B on top. It is important to get that B, since it is the third of the G major chord.

Leather Britches

3
G

Katy Hill

G
one passing note

Brickyard Joe

G

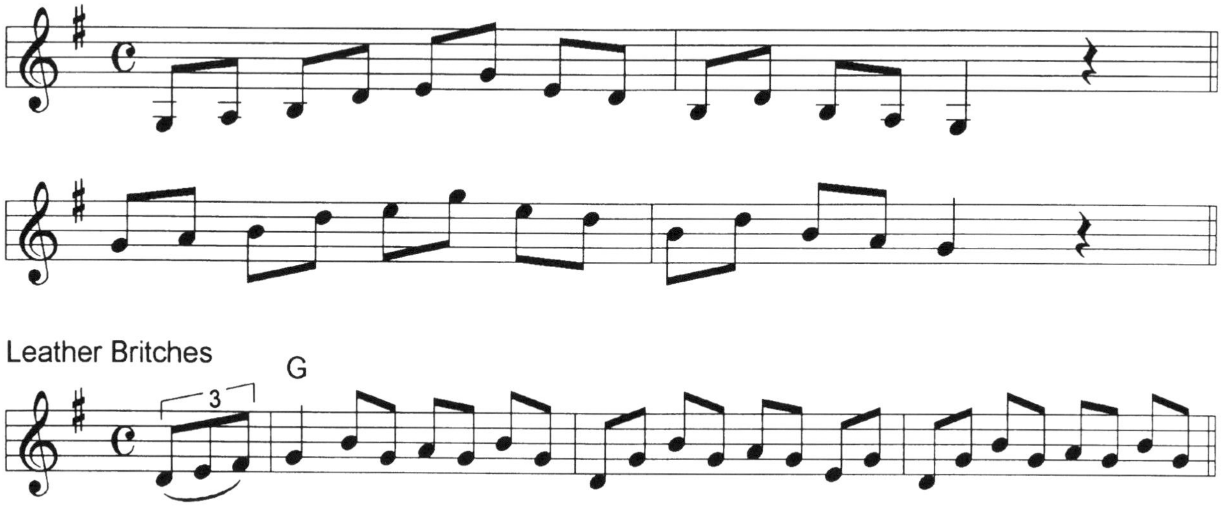

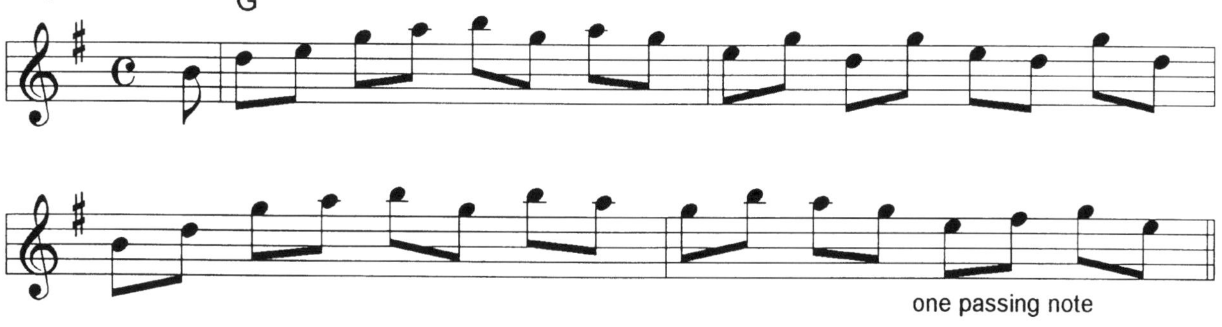

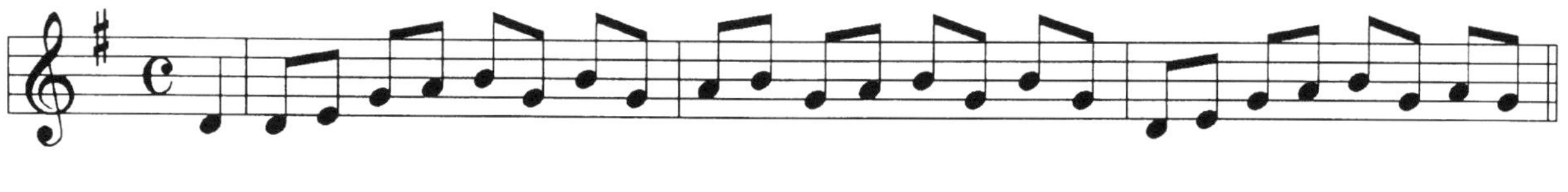

In that last example, notice that on the lower three strings, you play the open string, plus two fingered notes on each string. Regularity like that makes it easy to play scales quickly and smoothly. Try this:

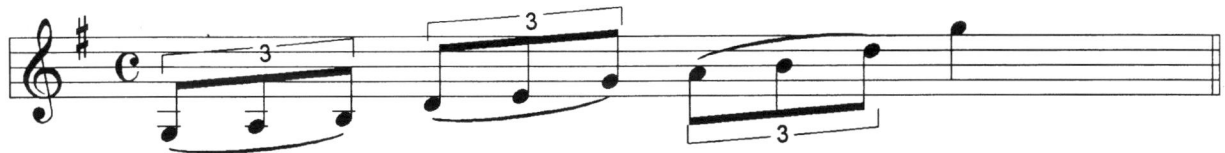

Now use the same notes for this flashy pickup measure. You don't have to really count the division of the pickup; just whip off the pattern on one fast bow stroke.

Hokum.

Now a few more G major pentatonic examples. These are all melodic patterns, which can get pretty boring if you overdo it, but are very satisfying if played in moderation.

Now you either need to practice the G major pentatonic scale by ear, or, if you want some structure, here is another hornpipe type G triad arpeggio:

Here is the same arpeggio, alternated with measures of G major pentatonic. Play your own runs.

Combining Scales

Before we go to the G major scale, we will pause and do an exercise combining scales and triads. We will play the exercise in the key G major. We will play alternating measures of G major and D major chords. We will use the G major triad and the G major pentatonic scale over the G chord, and the D major triad and D major pentatonic scale over the D chord.

As you all recall, our basic chords are formed by starting on a note in a scale, and playing every other note, for a total of the three notes. If you do that on each of the seven notes of the major scale, you get three major triads, I, IV, and V; three minor triads, ii, iii, and vi; and one diminished triad, vii-diminished. In the key of G major, G is the I chord, and the D is the V chord.

In the preceding section on D major sounds, I told you that the D major triad and the D major pentatonic scale could be used over any D major chord, in whatever key that D major chord might be found. We now find our D major chord in the key of G.

V-I - The Bedrock of Western Music

Our exercise has alternating measures of G major and D major, or I and V, in the key of G major. This progression, (I)-V-I has been chosen because it is the most important chord progression in the major scale. There is a special relationship between a note and the note a perfect fifth above it, such as G up to D. This relationship has been recognized by most human cultures. The perfect fifth is the second note in the overtone series, after the octave. Use of the perfect fifth as a harmony note is very widespread, and was one of the very first harmonies used in Western music. Major and minor chords all have a perfect fifth above the root. The interval of a perfect fifth is considered the most stable, except the octave. And so on. A great deal of Western music, symphonies to popular songs, can be analyzed as movement from I to V, and back again. Many, many fiddle tunes are just I-V-I. The progression V-I produces a feeling of expectation and fulfillment because of two elements: root movement down a perfect fifth to tonic (first scale degree), and the leading tone. The 7th scale degree of the major scale is called the leading tone, because it is a half step below tonic, and the ear, having become accustomed to tonic as the home note or tonal center, expects the leading tone to, well, *lead* to tonic. The 7th scale degree is the third of the V chord. In our present example, we are in the key of G. The 7th scale degree, or leading tone, is F♯, the 3rd of the D chord.

We will start by alternating triads, to tune our ears up, and then mix in pentatonic scales. So we will alternate measures of G major triad (G, B, D), with measures of D major triad (D, F♯, A).

Easy spagheesie. And rocking back and forth between those two basic arpeggios is very satisfying. Just a word about connecting runs. To play flowing solos, you need to be able to enter a scale at any point; that is to say, be able to start playing a triad, or a scale, such as our pentatonic scales, on any chord tone or scale degree. When you are learning scales and apeggios, there is a tendency to start playing the run from the root, or first note. Starting on the root is often boring and you cannot smoothly connect runs unless you have many pathways into your scales. A few more examples, then you should play alternating G and D arpeggios by ear.

Now we will mix in the G major pentatonic scale (G, A, B, D, E) and D major pentatonic scale (D, E, F#, A, B):

Now it's time for you to practice alternating measures of G major and D major on your own.

G Major Scale

First, a few excerpts, using the G major scale, G, A, B, C, D, E, F♯, over the I chord, G major.

Twinkle Little Star

Turkey in the Straw

Nelson's Victory Hornpipe

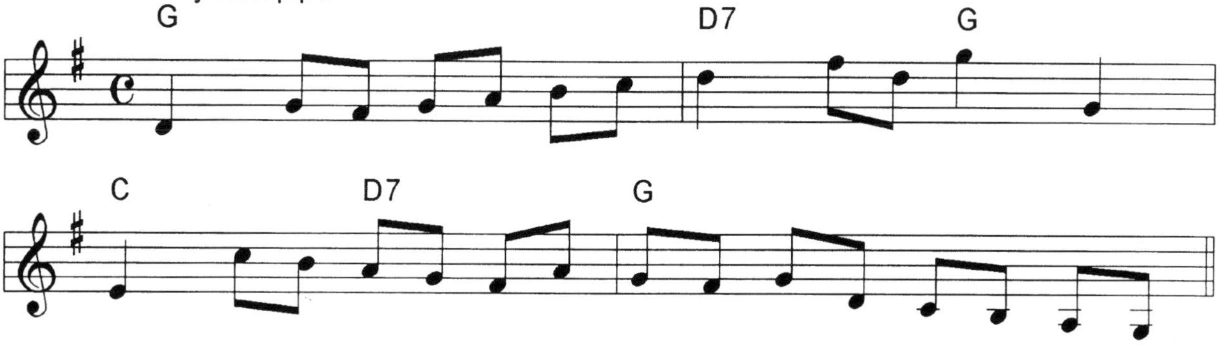

Now our regular old violin lesson type scale exercises:

Here are the triads (basic three note chords) built on each scale degree:

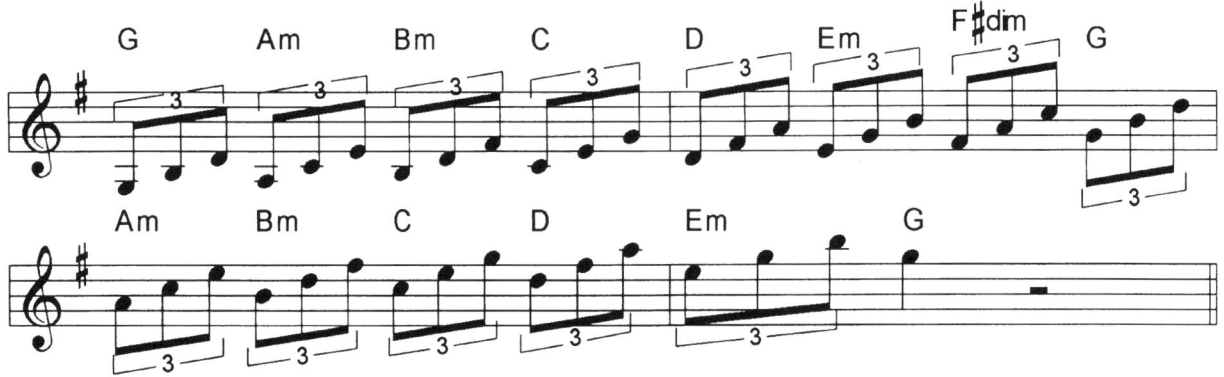

Seventh chord arpeggios:

Major Seventh Sound

Here are a few measures emphasizing the major seventh scale degree, F♯:

Here is the same jazz vamp we used in D; this time in G. Try out the major seventh sound.

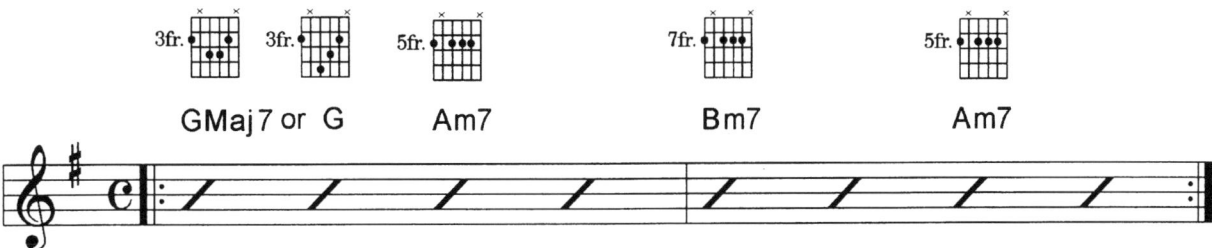

A Major

We now turn to A major.

First, the A major triad: A, C♯, E.

Then A major pentatonic: A, B, C♯, E, F♯.

Finally, the A major scale: A, B, C♯, D, E, F♯, G♯.

A Major Triad

A Major Pentatonic

A Major Pentatonic

Here is a diagram of the A major pentatonic scale, spelled A, B, C♯, E, F♯, over two octaves. Notice that only the A and E strings are played open.

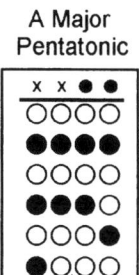

A few repertoire excerpts with the A major pentatonic scale:

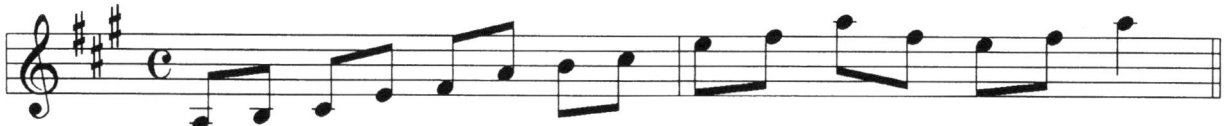

Sally Goodin'

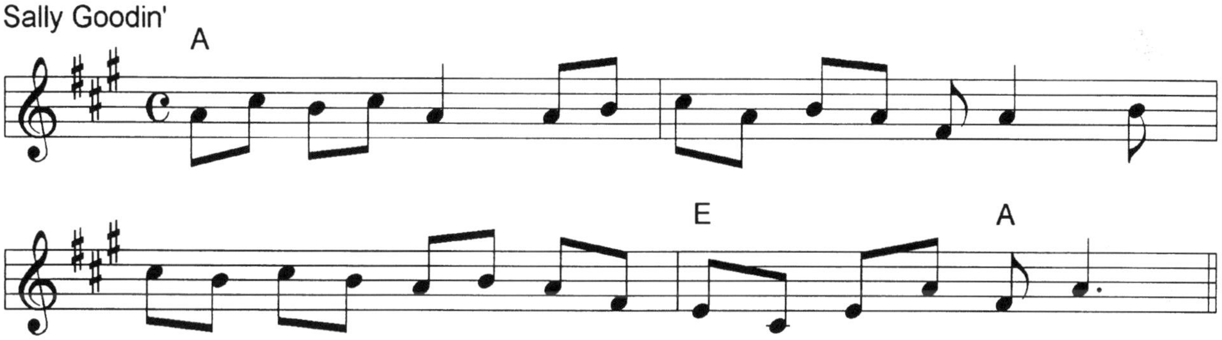

Salt River

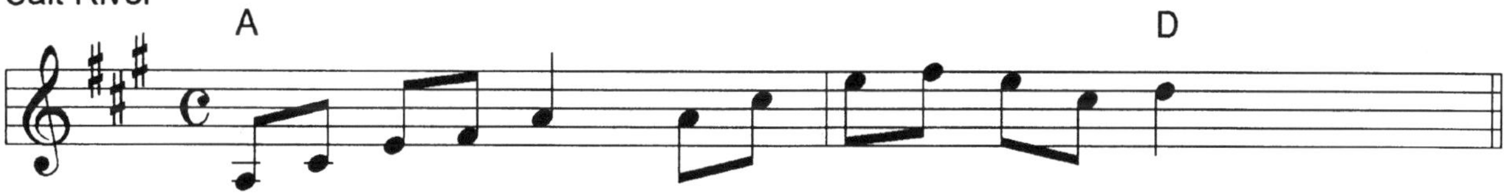

Cotton Eyed Joe

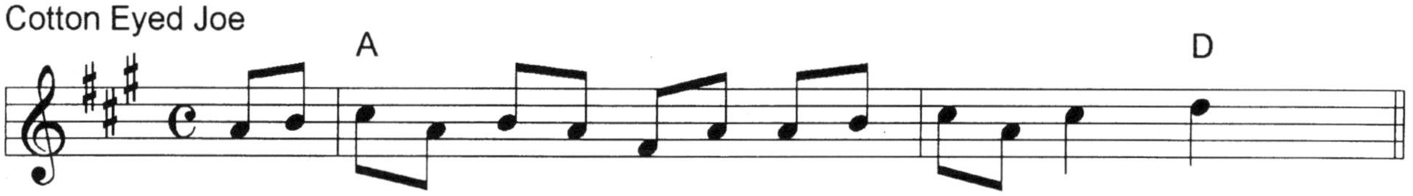

Grey Eagle

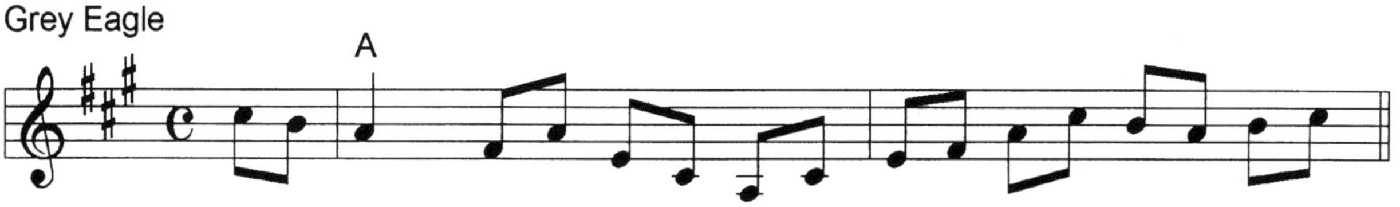

Having worked this far, you no longer need the structure of our "Write Your Own Hornpipe" introductory arpeggio. Just play around with the A major pentatonic scale by ear, and substitute some measures of A major pentatonic over some A chords in tunes you now play, no matter what key.

Combining Scales - I-IV-V

As you recall, there are three major triads in the major scale, I, IV and V. For our first exercise in combining scales, we used I and V. We now add the IV chord. Since we have only studied D major, G major, and are in the middle of A major, we are going to have to do this exercise in D major. This is because I, IV and V in D major are D, G, and A. So we will immediately move our A major materials from the key of A, and use the A major triad and A major pentatonic in the key of D, where A functions as the V chord. We will begin with triads, and then move on to pentatonic scales.

Now let's play the same chord progression, I-IV-V-I, using the D major pentatonic (D, E, F#, A, B), G major pentatonic (G, A, B, D, E), and A major pentatonic, (A, B, C#, E, F#).

Pleasant enough, but frankly, all those pentatonic scales sound a little bland. Now is the time for you to practice the chord progression on your own. There is no reason why you shouldn't use the D major scale over both the D chord and the G chord, and add the note G to the A pentatonic scale to give it an A7 sound. One example follows at the top of the next page.

A Major Scale

First a few excerpts using the A major scale, A, B, C#, D, E, F#, G#, over the I chord, A:

Devil's Dream

Jack of Diamonds

Fire on the Mountain

Now our scale exercises:

Major Seventh Sound

Here are a few examples emphasizing the major seventh, G♯ in the key of A major:

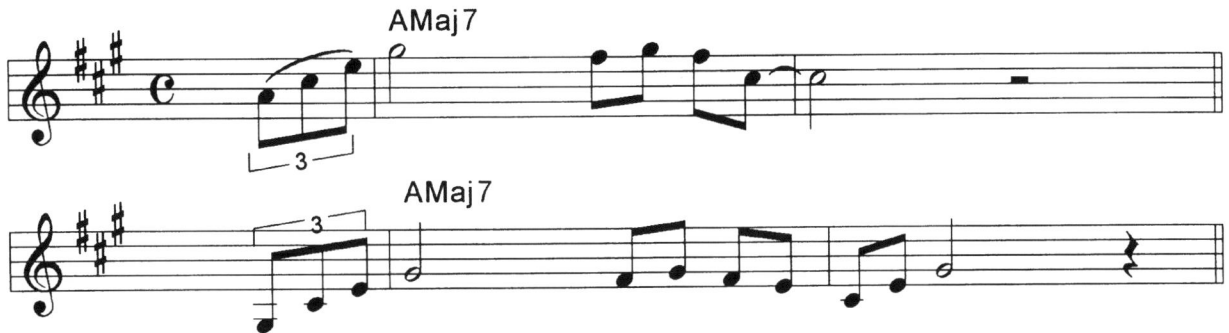

Here is our jazz vamp, this time in A major, and expanded to a more complete progression. Just noodle around with the A major scale.

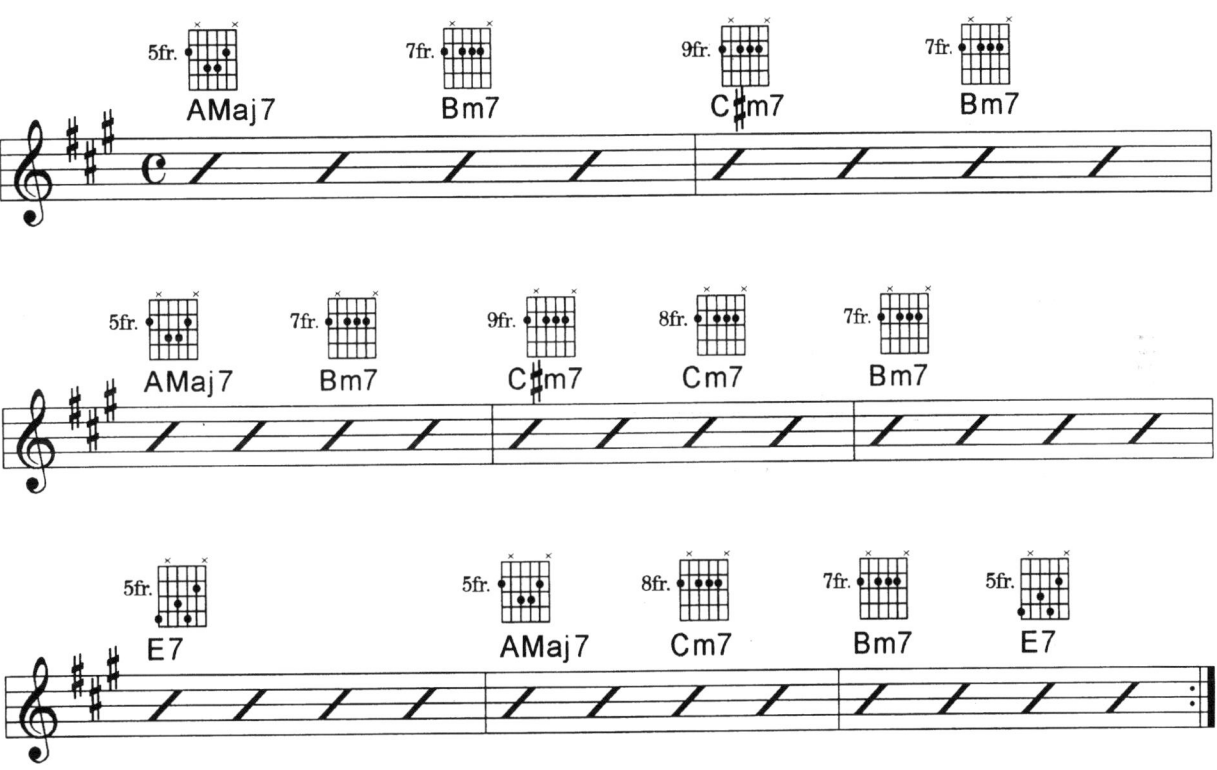

C Major

We will start with the C major triad: C, E, G.

Then we will look at the C major pentatonic scale: C, D, E, G, A.

Then we will have exercises combining chords and scales.

Finally, we will learn the C major scale: C, D, E, F, G, A, B.

C Major Triad

Notice that the first example is the same closed position major triad shape we noted in G (p.18), and it is also found in D with its root on the A string. The second example is the same shape, but with the open E string replacing a stopped note. Continuing on:

stretch up there

Now a few of our familiar hornpipe arpeggio examples:

Peerless Hornpipe

Chandler's Hornpipe

Belle of Claremont Hornpipe

C Major Pentatonic

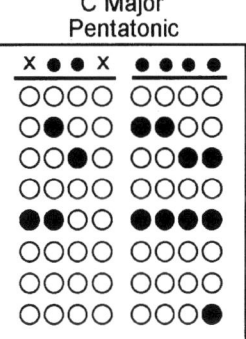

Here is the C major pentatonic scale, C, D, E, G, A. The diagram on the left shows the scale over one octave, and the diagram on the right shows the scale extended up and down a few notes. Note how, in the diagram on the right, the fingerings are the same for the G and D strings, and the A and E strings (except for that high C).

Here are the patterns written out:

Our examples from the repertoire aren't that great. The key of C is not nearly as common a fiddle key as D, G, and A. The best known tunes in C are *Wagoner* and *Billy in the Low Ground*. *Wagoner* is basically just the C major triad plus one A, and *Billy in the Low Ground* is C major pentatonic plus one B used as a decorative note.

Wagoner

Billy in the Low Ground

Amin

More C major pentatonic examples:

As always, you should play around with the C major pentatonic scale on your own.

Combining Scales - I-IV-V

Now we are going to do a three chord exercise, like we did in the middle of the A major chapter. We will play the same progression, I-IV-V-I, this time in the key of G major. In G major, the chords are G-C-D-G. The C major triad will be functioning as the IV chord.

We start with triads. Remember, we are now in the key of G.

Now the same progression with major pentatonic scales.

Try it on your own.

Mixolydian Exercise - I-VII

One more exercise with our C major triad and C major pentatonic scale before we move on to the C major scale. This exercise will use the C chord functioning as the VII chord in D mixolydian. We don't need to worry about knowing mixolydian at this point. Just play the D major triad and D major pentatonic over the D chord, and the C major triad and C major pentatonic over the C chord. Note the key signature, with one sharp, normally means G major, but is also the proper key signature for D mixolydian.

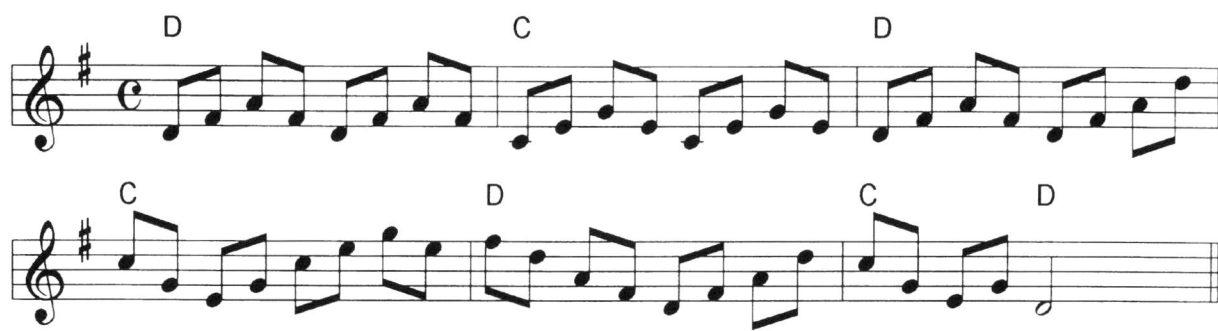

C Major Scale

One repertoire excerpt:

Hit or Miss Reel

C major scale exercises:

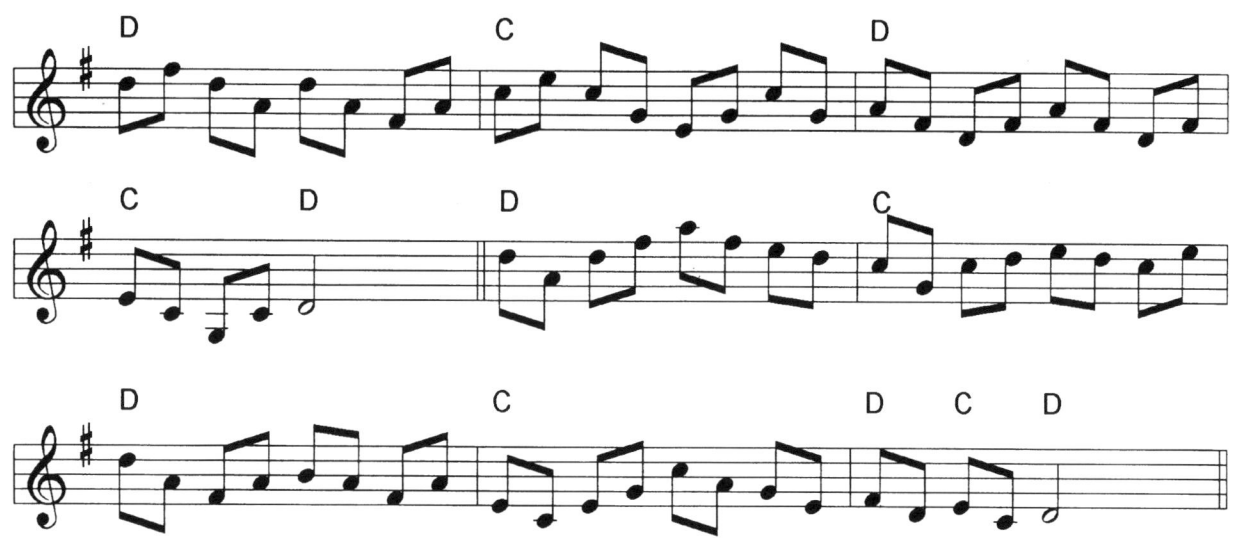

Triad arpeggios:

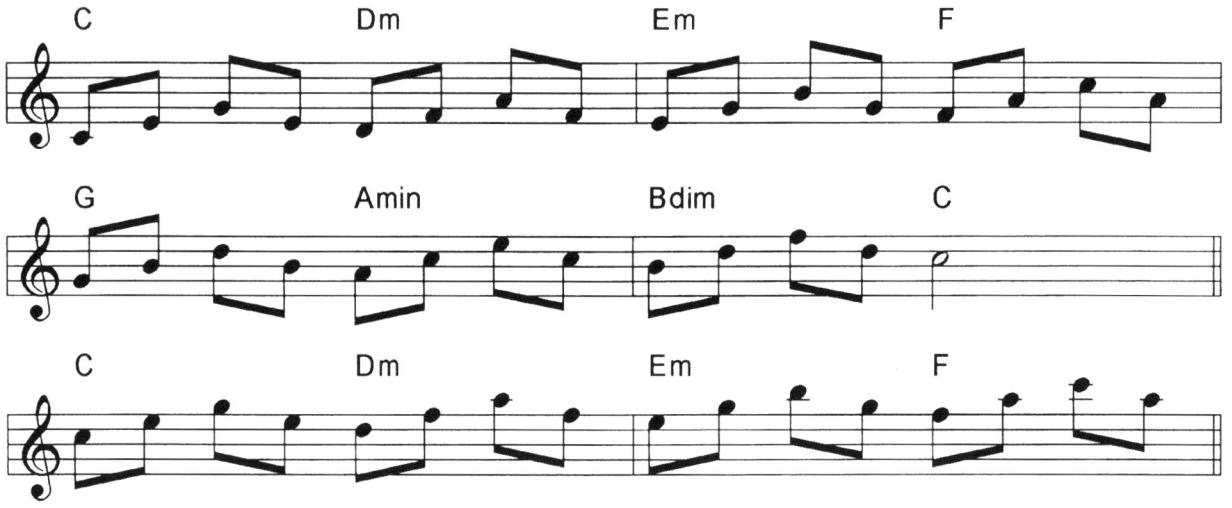

Seventh chord arpeggios:

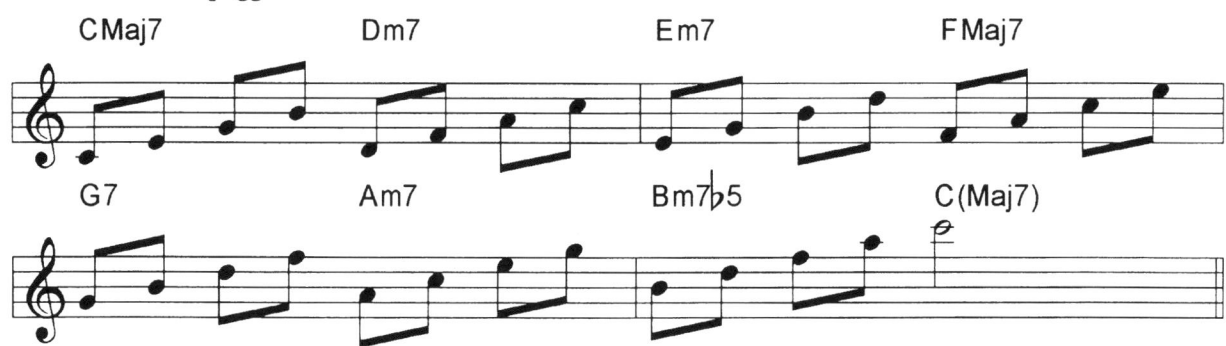

Major Seventh Sound

Here are a few examples emphasizing the major seventh, B, in the key of C major:

For your jazz vamp practice, have your guitar player move the chord progression in A up three frets, so it will be in C. Below is a new kind of vamp, this one utilizing what is called a circle of fifths progression. I suggest you try two things. One, noodle around the C major scale. Two, try playing the arpeggio or pentatonic scale over the respective chords, like C major pentatonic over the C chord, A major pentatonic over the A7 chord, etc. You can have your accompanist double the duration of the chords if you want.

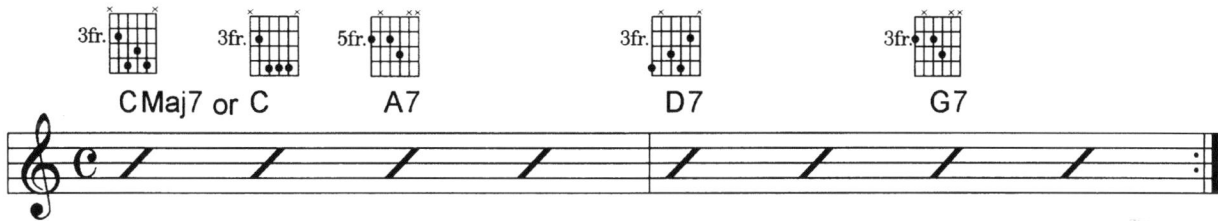

F Major

We are getting out of our core fiddle keys, but there are a number of tunes in F, including rags such as *The Beaumont Rag*. And you will need the F major triad and pentatonic scale over F chords in many keys, notably for us, F functioning as the IV chord in C major. So we will take a quick look.

First, the F major triad, F, A, C:

Here is the F major triad functioning as IV in the key of C major:

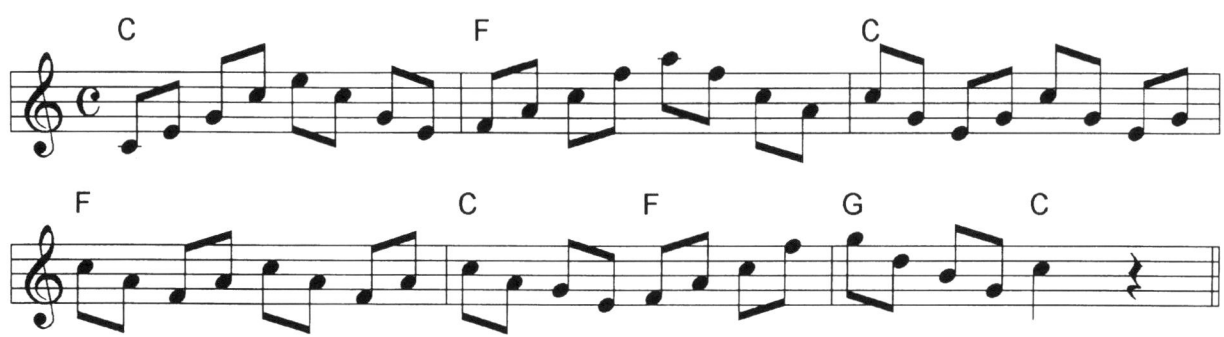

F Major Pentatonic

The F major pentatonic scale is spelled F, G, A, C, D.

Here are a few measures of I-IV in the key of C major, using the F major pentatonic over the F chord, which is functioning as the IV chord.

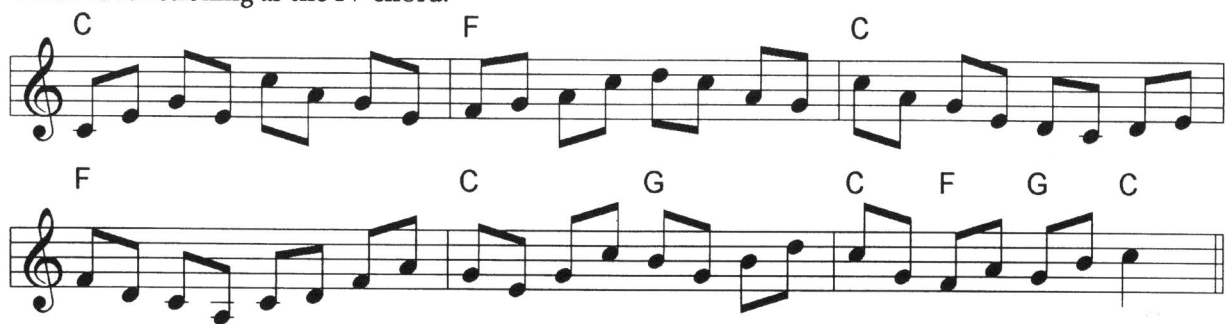

F Major Scale

Here, without examples or exercises, is the F major scale: F, G, A, B♭, C, D, E:

B♭ Major

The IV chord in the key of F major is B♭. Here is the B♭ major triad, B♭, D, F; and the B♭ major pentatonic scale, B♭, C, D, F, G. Both are notated in F major.

I will leave it to you to do some of our chord combining exercises in F, if you are so inclined.

E Major

There are almost no fiddle tunes in E major, but it is a very important key in other styles, such as country and folk (The People's Key). E is also the V chord in A major, so we need to know the major triad and major pentatonic for that function, at least. Here is the E major triad: E, G#, B, and the E major pentatonic scale: E, F#, G#, B, C#:

E Major Triad

E Major Pentatonic

Here is the E major triad functioning as V in this I-V chord progression in A major:

Here is I-V in A major, using the E major pentatonic over the V chord:

E Major Scale

Here, without examples, is the E major scale: E, F♯, G♯, A, B, C♯, D♯:

Note that the E major scale, from the note E on the D string, is the same pattern as A major, starting from A on the G string.

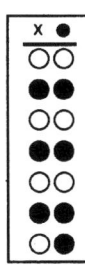

Dominants

Now we look at dominant chords and the dominant scale.

Generally, the chords used to accompany traditional music are plain old three note triads. An exception is the V chord. The V chord is often played, or could be played, as a seventh chord, meaning is it has an interval of a seventh played above the root, in addition to the 1, 3, 5 of the basic triad. If you build a seventh chord on the fifth scale degree of the major scales, you get a major triad with a 10 half step ♭7 (you recall that a seventh chord built on the first scale degree of the major scale has an 11 half step major seventh on top, as does the seventh chord build on the fourth scale degree; see page 17).

The V chord is called the dominant chord, because the fifth scale degree of the major scale is called the dominant (the first scale degree is called the tonic, and the fourth is called the subdominant). The V7 chord is called the dominant seventh chord, and any chord with that formula, 1, 3, 5, ♭7, is termed a dominant seventh chord, usually shortened to "seventh chord."

You recall that the chord progression V-I is considered the fundamental major scale chord progression, and that its feeling of expectation and fulfillment comes from two elements: root movement down a perfect fifth; and the leading tone (3rd of the V chord is a half step below tonic). The V7 adds another element: the highly discordant tritone (♭5), formed between the 3rd of the V chord, and its ♭7, which demands resolution. For example, the G7 chord is spelled: G, B, D, F, and the tritone is between B and F. In medieval church music, the tritone was not allowed, being dubbed *diabolus in musicum*, or devil in music. The first accidental was B♭, used to avoid that very tritone between B and F.

V7 is the only naturally occuring dominant seventh chord in the major scale. However, it is very common for major key tunes to use dominant chords whose roots are other scale degrees, namely II7, VI7, and less often III7, rather than the naturally occuring ii7, vi7, and iii7. These are called secondary dominants. So we need to be able to play the seventh chord arpeggio as automatically as we can now play major triads and major pentatonics.

We will also learn the dominant scale, which is the same as a major scale, but with a ♭7 scale degree. Same ♭7 as the dominant chord, right? This scale naturally occurs beginning on the fifth scale degree of the major scale, but we need to learn it, not as part of the major scale, but as a scale in its own right, so we can play over any dominant chord, no matter what key it appears in.

The dominant scale is the same as the mixolydian mode, so you will kind of get double duty from your effort, although the musical function of the two scales really makes them feel different, and merits separate study and consideration. I will say now that what we are learning as the dominant scale is known by almost the whole rest of the world as the mixolydian scale. I think it is useful to make a distinction between its true modal use as mixolydian, and its V7 function in the major scale; therefore, I do.

A Dominant

We begin our study of dominants with A dominant sounds. We will start with the A7 chord, then look at the A dominant scale. We will first learn the A7 chord and A dominant scale in the key of D major, because that is the key in which they naturally occur. We will then move the chord and scale to the key of G, and show their application there.

A Seventh Chord

The A seventh chord is spelled A, C#, E, G.

Here are a couple of repertoire excerpts with the A7 chord. In the first, we have one extra note, F#.

Tommorow Morning

In *Soldier's Joy*, we don't get the whole A7 chord; just the 5, E, and the b7, G, are present.

Soldier's Joy

Now a few examples, alternating the D major triad and the A7 chord, I and V7 in the key of D.

The above exercise is like the first ones we did combining scales, but now using the A7 chord where before we have used the A major triad. Play this progression on your own a little, and use the A major triad some, and see how the sound is different from A7.

Note this shape, which is a dominant seventh chord with the root as the bottom note, like A7 starting on the G string. This shape could be played with the root of the seventh chord falling under the first or second finger, on the G, D, or A strings. That is a lot of root notes. Remembering this shape can help orient you as you move rapidly through a series of seventh chords.

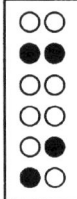

A Dominant Scale

The A dominant scale is spelled A, B, C♯, D, E, F♯, G, so it is like the A major scale with G instead of G♯.

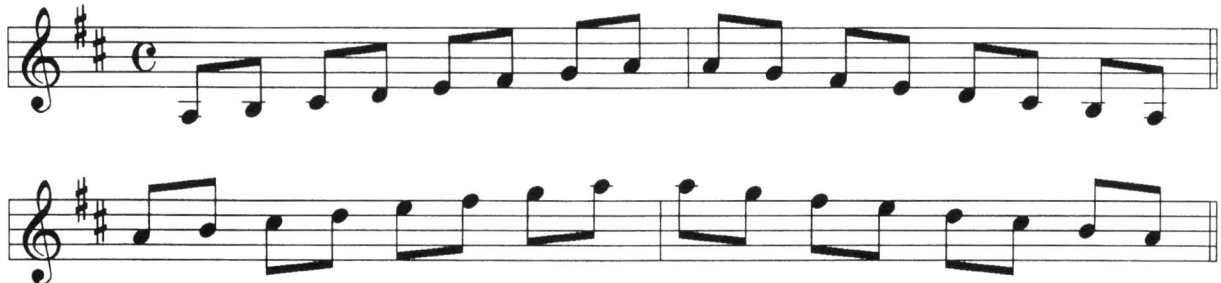

Here are a few V7-I runs, A7-D in the key of D major, using the A dominant scale:

A couple of comments. First: in the above examples, you are obviously just playing the D major scale. Its a matter of which notes of the D scale. The A7 runs start on A7 chord tones, and have chord tones, A, C♯, E, G, on most of the beats. That's why they are heard as A dominant runs.

Second: In the section on major sounds we just used major triads and major pentatonic scales over the V chords. Now we are using V7 and the dominant seventh scale. These new materials are not necessarily better, just different. Compare the following A major pentatonic run and A dominant seventh scale run:

There is definitely a difference, but it's really just a matter of choice and style. The major pentatonic scale will always fit over a 7th chord, but it doesn't have the ♭7, so it lacks the spice. On the other hand, the pentatonic scale has that nice, pleasing, open sound. As you like it.

Secondary Dominants - II7-V7-(I)

V7 is the only naturally occurring dominant seventh chord in the major scale. Sometimes, however, progressions use dominant seventh chords built on notes other than the fifth scale degree. These are called secondary dominants. The idea is that any chord in the progression can be preceeded by its own V7 chord, or properly speaking, by a dominant seventh chord built on the note a perfect fifth above the root of the chord in question. One of the most basic examples of the principle is preceding the V7 chord with its own V7 chord, which works out to be a dominant seventh chord built on the second scale degree, and hence called II7, although the academics would call it V7 of V7, or V7/V7.

The progression goes II7-V7-I. The repertoire examples which follow have a cadence (musical pause), on V7, before proceeding to I at the beginning of the (omitted) next phrase.

Our A7 chord is the II7 in the key of G. So we are taking the A7 out of the key of D major, where it functioned as V7, and are moving it to function as II7 in the key of G.

You don't really get much sense of the A7 chord; it could just as well be A minor. Here is the chord change fleshed out a little:

In the next example, the II7 makes its appearance in the next to last measure. At some point you will start to recognize the common accidentals indicating secondary dominants, like the C♯ in the key of G signals the A7 chord, II7 in the key of G.

Twinkle Little Star

We will now do a II7-V7-I exercise. We will use our A7 functioning as II7 in the key of G major. Our progression will go I-IV-II7-V7, or G-C-A7-D7. We will start with G and C major triads, and the A7 arpeggio. We will just use half notes for the D7 chord, since we haven't learned D7 yet.

Here is the same progression, I-IV-II7-V7 in the key of G, using the A dominant scale, A, B, C♯, D, E, F♯, G. Since D7 will be the next seventh chord we study, I have also used the D7 arpeggio: D, F♯, A, C.

Try it on your own.

D Dominant

D Seventh Chord

The D7 chord is spelled D, F#, A, C. It is the V7 chord in the key of G major, so we look at the arpeggio, and have our first examples, notated in that key.

Please memorize.

Now a few I-V7 examples, using the G major triad and the D7 chord:

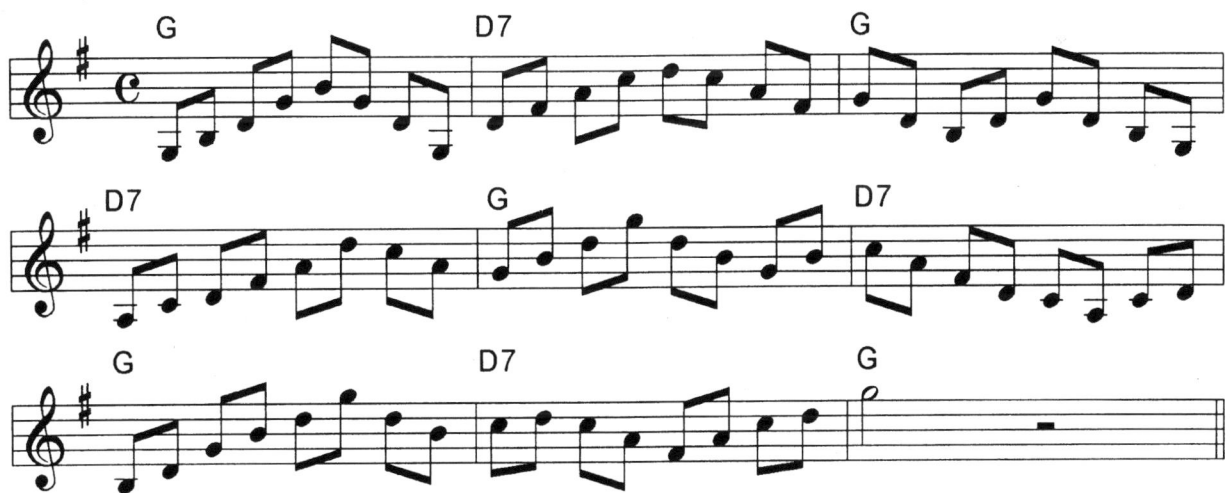

II7-V7-(I)

Now let's take our D7 arpeggio out of the key of G major, and move it to C major, where it functions as II7 in the following I-IV-II7-V7 progression:

D Dominant Scale

The D dominant scale is spelled D, E, F#, G, A, B, C, so it is the same as the D major scale with C rather than C#. We will first look at the scale in G major, where it occurs naturally.

Now a few examples, alternating I-V, using G runs and D dominant runs:

$II^7 - V^7 - (I)$

Now let's move our D dominant scale to the key of C, and use it over D7 functioning as II7 in our I-IV-II7-V7 progression:

G Dominant

G Seventh Chord

The G seventh chord is spelled G, B, D, F. It is the V7 chord in the key of C, so our first examples are in that key.

Now a few measures, alternating C triads with the G7 arpeggio:

In the preceeding sections on A and D dominants, we moved the seventh chords to function as II7. We will not do that with G7. G7 is the II7 chord in the key of F major. At this point, I am certain you can easily learn G7 as II7 of F on your own, when you need to. And I want to keep working with A7, D7, and G7, which we will combine in one progression, as soon as we take a quick look at the G dominant scale.

G Dominant Scale

The G dominant scale is spelled G, A, B, C, D, E, F, so it is like the G major scale with F instead of F♯. It occurs naturally in the key of C, so we first look at it notated in that key.

Here is I-V7, with the C major, and the G dominant scale. I know, its all the C major scale.

Now, if you are really diligent, you will put some D dominant and G dominant scales in our I-IV-II7-V7 progression:

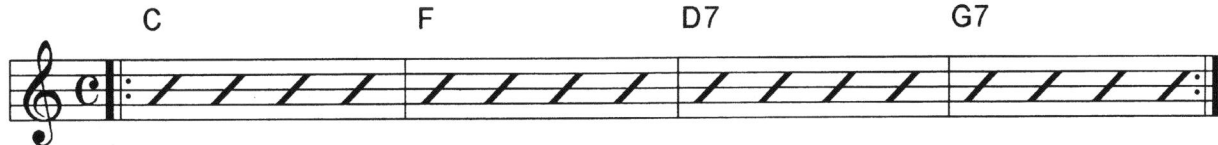

Secondary Dominants - I-VI7-II7-V7-I

We have seen how V7 can be proceeded by its own V7, namely II7. Similarly, II7 can be preceded by its own V7, which works out to be VI7. It is often seen in a very common swing and rag progression, I-VI7-II7-V7-I. We will play the progression in C major, and use the three dominant scales we have learned so far (watch the accidentals-they only apply to the end of the measure).

Ain't that fun?

C Dominant

C Seventh Chord

C7 is spelled C, E, G, B♭. It naturally occurs in the key of F major, and we will look at it first in that key.

We will just have one little example of C7 functioning as V7 in the key of F major. To be honest, I have mixed feelings about slighting F major in this book. But you have to draw the line somewhere, and F just gets too far afield of the core keys. There, I've gotten it off my chest.

C Dominant Scale

The C dominant scale is spelled C, D, E, F, G, A, B♭, so it is the same as the C major scale with B♭ instead of B. We look at it in F major, where it naturally occurs.

I7

Another secondary dominant is I7. The IV chord can be preceeded by its V7, and that works out to be I7. Here are a couple of examples:

Here is an example of G7 functioning as I7 in the key of G major, going to the IV chord, C:

Dominant Scale Blues Playing

Although it is not an old time sound, the I dominant and IV dominant scales can be used for blues or blues based playing. This is very common in Swing Era playing, and is one the basic jazz sounds to this day. Our example is in G major with C as the IV chord. We are using dominant scales, not for their dominant function, but simply for the jangly sound.

Mixing in some b3rds in addition to, or instead of, the major 3rd of the chords fills out the dominant blues sound.

A lot of Swing Era playing uses the major scale, but mixes in b7s and b3rds as *blue notes*, so you get an effect much like the above example.

E Dominant

E Seventh Chord

The E7 chord is spelled E, G#, B, D. It occurs naturally in the key of A, so we notate it in that key first. Note the same finger pattern as we looked at with A7, on page 50.

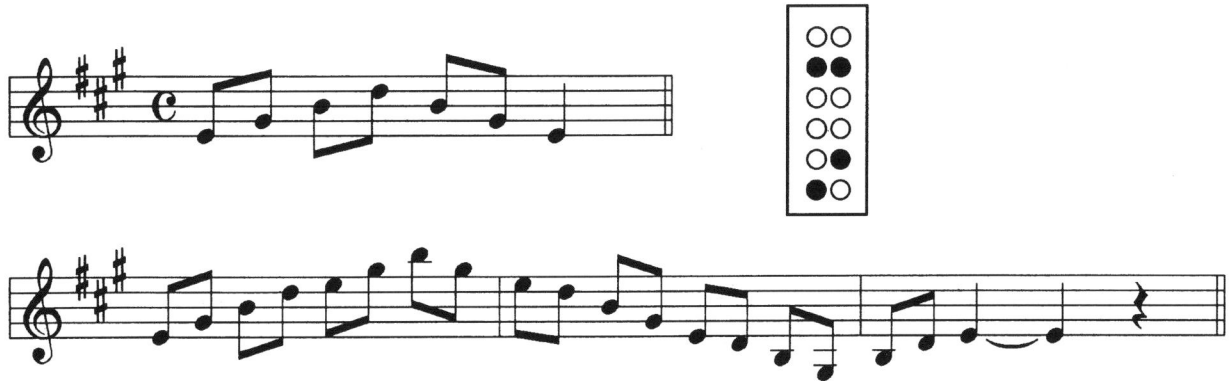

Here are a few examples of E7 functioning as V7 in the key of A major.

E Dominant Scale

The E dominant scale is spelled E, F#, G#, A, B, C#, D, so it is like the E major scale with D instead of D#.

A few examples of the E dominant scale over E7, functioning as V7, in this I-V7-I progression:

You should probably play around with that a little.

II7-V7-(I)

Now let's return to our I-IV-II7-V7 progression, this time in the key of D major, where E7 functions as II7.

(more I-IV-II7-V7)

I-VI7-II7-V7

We now move our E dominant scale to the key of G, where it functions as VI7 in our good time turnaround progression, I-VI7-II7-V7-I:

B Dominant

B7 is the V7 of the key of E major, and as such, is a little out of our core traditional keys, but you need to be able to play in E, and the B7 is useful in the core keys, as II7 in A, and VI7 in D.

B Seventh Chord

B7 is spelled B, F#, D#, A. We look at it first in E major, where it functions as V7. In the first example, you have the choice of either playing the D# with the little finger on the G string, or reaching down and getting it with the index finger on the D string.

B Dominant Scale

The B dominant scale is spelled B, C#, D#, E, F#, G#, A. Here is the scale, notated still in E major:

I-V7-(I)

A few measures of the B dominant scale functioning as V7 in the key of E major:

II7-V7-(I)

Now let's look at B7 functioning as II7 in the key of A major. I have eliminated the IV chord from the progression we have been using, so it is now I-II7-V7.

I-VI7-II7-V7

Finally, we move our B7 to the key of D, where it functions as VI7 in our I-VI7-II7-V7 progression:

Extended and Altered Dominants

9ths, 11ths, & 13ths

If you look outside traditional music, you will notice chords named 9th, 11th, and 13th. You should know what that means, and how to handle these chords. Our basic chord building method is to stack up thirds, or skipping every other note, and we have gotten up to 1-3-5-7. We are studying dominant chords, which means 1-3-5-b7. To that formula, we can keep on going, and add a 9th (which is the same as the 2nd scale degree), an 11th (same as 4th), and a 13th (same as 6th). After that, the notes start repeating. (And you would have all the notes of the dominant scale.) **These higher extensions of the chord do not change its function; they just add color.** That is, A7, A9 and A13 all serve the same musical function as dominant chords. As a single line instrument, you will just be playing the dominant scale, and don't need to worry about those color tones the accompaniment is playing.

Altered Dominants

You also see chords with names like A7b9+, and C7b5#9b9. What the heck is that all about? Quite simply, in jazz, dominant chord are often altered for more expressive colors. Most often, altered dominants are described as dominant chords with #9 and/or b9 instead of the major 9th; and/or #5 and/or b5 in addition to the prefect 5th, or instead of the perfect 5th (note that #5 is the same note as b13th, and you will see it written both ways). You will also see #11 chords. In playing dominant chords, the 11th is almost always sharped, on the infrequent occasions it is used (don't confuse that with the suspended chord, where 4 [same as 11] replaces 3 in the chord).

As a single line instrument, you can pretty much play the dominant scale, with any or no alterations, no matter which exact variation of the chord is being played or called for. That statement is a little overbroad, but not much. When you play music in which these colors are acceptable, a wide range of dissonance is okay. So that means if the chord indicated is C7b5, you can play a C7b9+ run, or the C dominant scale, or any other alteration of the dominant scale.

These sounds are not necessarily weird. Here is one example in the key of D, starting with the V7 chord, A7. We will play the #5, E#, and the b9, Bb. It's not that far out; it just sounds a little bluesy. Note that the #5, E#, could also have been spelled as a b13, F.

Flat 5th Substitution

Going way overboard on this stuff, but so you will know: For a dominant chord, you can substitute a dominant chord or run a tritone (♭5th [or ♯4]) away. (Up or down, it's the same note.) Altered or not, as you like. Example, for G7 going to C, you could play a D♭7 run for the last part of the G7 chord. It works because the 3 and ♭7 of one chord is the ♭7 and 3 of the other chord.

I will give one example, since it also gives me a chance to push my little shapes on you. We are in the key of D major, starting on the V7, A7. The first measure is a straight A7 run. The second measure is an E♭7 run, the flat five substitute for A7. Notice that the E♭7 run is just that same dominant seventh shape we have used on A7 and E7, but starting with the root under the index finger playing E♭ on the D string.

Augmented Chords

Augmented chords almost always serve a dominant function, so I will mention them here. An augmented chord is spelled 1-3-♯5 and an augmented seventh chord is spelled 1-3-♯5-♭7. The ♯5 just adds a little unsettled feeling to the chord, but it still retains its dominant function. As a single line instrument, you can simply add the ♯5 to the dominant scale, in addition to, or instead of, the perfect 5th. The symbol for augmented chords is Aug. or +.

Dominants in Minor Keys

Will be discussed with the minor scale, later in the book.

IV Chord - Lydian

I'm kidding, right? Mostly. Again I tell you, there are three major triads in the major scale, I, IV, and V. We have concentrated on I and V, learning to play the major scale and its included triad and pentatonic scale. Then we learned dominants. Along the way, we have played the IV chord, and I have said play either the IV triad, or IV pentatonic, and finally I have said to just go ahead and play I major, the key you are playing in. I just want to discuss it all in one place.

Why do I say lydian? I will explain, and then tell you to forget it. If you are playing in a major key, and you continue to play that major scale when playing over the IV chord, you will be playing the lydian scale as to the IV chord. An example makes it clear. If you are playing in the key of G major, which has one sharp, namely F♯, and you play that G major scale over the IV chord, C, let's see what you get. From C up an octave to the next C, using the notes of the G major scale, is C, D, E, F♯, G, A, B, (C). That looks just like the C major scale, but with a raised 4th scale degree, F♯ instead of F. And that is what the lydian scale is: same as a major scale but with a raised 4th scale degree. And so, if we were really taking a strict chord scale approach, changing scales with every chord change, we would have to learn the lydian scale on all the roots of common chords that might function as IV chords in fiddle tunes. But we are not that strict. It just makes more sense to play melodically in the key we are playing in. Fiddle tunes don't emphasize the lydianness of playing the I major scale over the IV chord. The IV pentatonic avoids the issue by omitting the 4th scale degree, and of course, the notes of the IV pentatonic scale are contained within I major.

What you don't play, if you want to sound traditional, is IV major scale. It doesn't sound bad, but it makes it seem like there has been a real tonal shift to the IV major scale, which is not traditional. Try it; it's all a matter of taste and style.

Over the IV chord you can play: (1) IV triad; (2) IV major pentatonic scale; (3) I major scale; (4) IV dominant scale, depending on style; (5) blues based runs, depending on style.

Here is one lydian scale example, to give the flavor of the sound. The example is C lydian, for which the proper key signature would be one sharp, F♯. I notated the example in C major, using the accidental to call your attention to the F♯, which gives the scale its lydian characteristic.

The scale sounds kind of enigmatic. Play around with it some rainy night.

Mixolydian

The mixolydian scale, or mode, is spelled 1, 2, 3, 4, 5, 6, ♭7, so it is the same as the major scale with ♭7 instead of major 7. The mixolydian mode is the same scale as we have just finished studying as the dominant scale, but it will feel very different as mixolydian. As the dominant scale, it was being used over a V7 chord in the major scale, which resolved down a fifth. Now it is the parent scale itself, built on the I chord. It is most commonly played starting on A and D; we will also look at E and G mixolydian. There is less ambiguity about which chord to play in mixolydian, compared with other modes, dorian and aeolian. The basic cadence is VII-I.

A Mixolydian

A mixolydian is spelled A, B, C♯, D, E, F♯, G, so it is the same as A major but with G instead of G♯. Its proper notation is with two sharps in the key signature. The basic chord progression is I-VII-I, or A-G-A. Often, however, mixolydian tunes may have major scale V7-I cadences, as well as, or instead of, modal VII-I cadences. *Old Joe Clark* illustrates this. The basic melody is clearly mixolydian, with the G♮. The first cadence, in the 4th measure, is usually played E7. The second cadence, measures 7-8, is sometimes played G-A, as in the first eight measures, or sometimes E7-A, as written the second time.

Old Joe Clark

This version of *Salt River* exhibits both VII (G) and V7 (E7). Note that it also has C♮ over the G chord. So on that long, two measure duration of G, this version uses the G major scale. Modal tunes don't always stay pure. This tune also has the IV chord, D, which is about the only other chord you see in mixolydian progressions; no secondary dominants.

Salt River

Here are a few scale examples. As you can see, the examples basically emphasize A major chord tones, then G major chord tones, filling in with the rest of the scale. I have put in a few E7's to contrast mixolydian and major.

D Mixolydian

D mixolydian is spelled D, E, F#, G, A, B, C, so it is the same as D major but with C instead of C#. The basic chord progression is D-C-D, with some A7's instead of C from time to time. (Just like the I-VII-I with some V7's we saw in A mixolydian.) The proper key signature is therefore one sharp, or you may see it notated as D major, two sharps, with C♮'s indicated to make it mixolydian.

E Mixolydian

E mixolydian is spelled E, F#, G#, A, B, C#, D. The basic I-VII-I chord progression is E-D-E. E mixolydian is not encountered as much as A and D mixolydian.

G Mixolydian

There's a little G mixolydian out there too. G mixolydian is spelled G, A, B, C, D, E, F, so it is like the G major scale with F instead of F♯. It is properly notated with no sharps or flats. The fundamental chord progression, I-VII-I, is G-F-G, and you will find some V7s (D7) also.

Pentatonics don't cut it

Here is that last example, played with the pentatonicky note E, rather than the defining mixolydian note, F, in the first measure. Sounds wimpy.

A Minor

We will start with the A minor triad: A, C, E. (The formula for a minor triad is 1, ♭3, 5.)

Then we will look at the A minor pentatonic scale: A, C, D, E, G.

Then we will look at the A aeolian scale: A, B, C, D, E, F, G, and
the A dorian scale: A, B, C, D, E, F♯, G.

Finally, we will look at modern uses of A minor sounds.

A Minor Triad

The A minor triad is spelled A, C, E. The key of A minor is the relative minor of C major, meaning they have the same key signature. Our first examples will be notated in A minor; no sharps or flats.

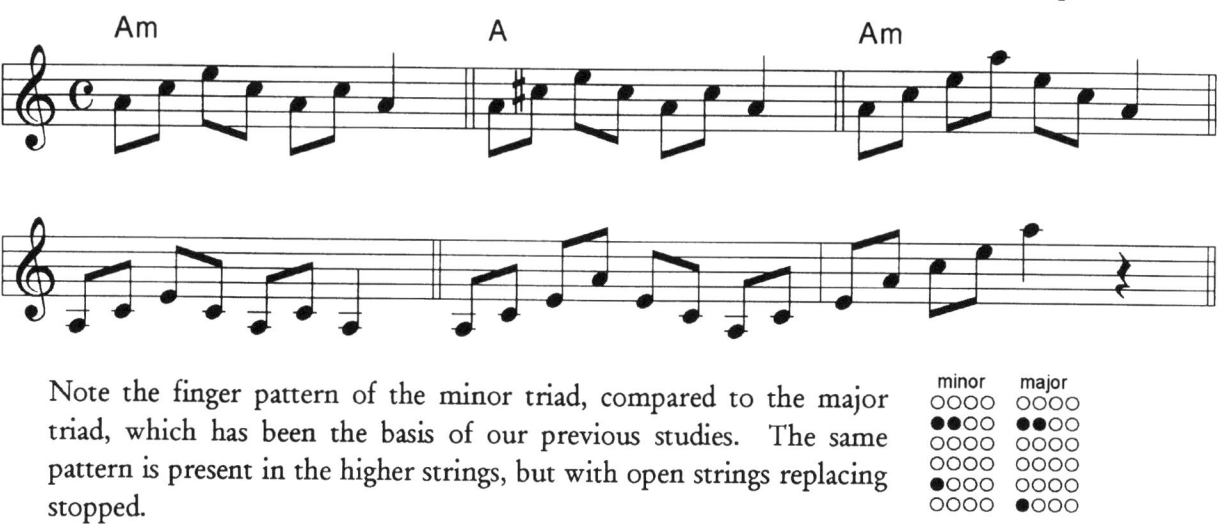

Note the finger pattern of the minor triad, compared to the major triad, which has been the basis of our previous studies. The same pattern is present in the higher strings, but with open strings replacing stopped.

Here is a basic minor modal progression i-VII-i, Am and G, using the Am triad:

Now let's take the Am triad out of its home key, and move it to a few other keys. You recall that in the major scale, there are three naturally occurring minor triads, with roots on the 2nd, 3rd, and 6th scale degrees. In the key of G major, Am is the ii chord, in this I-ii-V7-I progression.

In the key of C major, Am functions as the vi chord, in this I-vi-IV-V7-(I) progression.

Finally, one example of Am functioning as the iii chord in the key of F major. The progression is I-ii-iii-ii-I. You get the G minor triad, G, B♭, D, as a bonus.

A Minor Pentatonic

The minor pentatonic scale, like its relative major pentatonic scale, is of ancient folk origin, and should not be viewed as a subset of the minor scale. The scale has the same notes as its relative major, so, for example, the C major pentatonic scale and the A minor pentatonic scale have the same set of notes. In Am, the scale is A, C, D, E, G. The formula is 1, ♭3, 4, 5, ♭7.

Like its major pentatonic relative, the minor pentatonic scale can be used safely over (almost) any minor chord you will encounter. It is also very useful for blues playing. Millions and millions of records have been sold featuring rock guitar players blasting away with this scale over blues or rock progressions.

Here is the little finger pattern used to play the scale. It is just the same as C major pentatonic, but oriented from A to A.

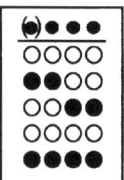

Here are a few examples:

We now use the A minor pentatonic in a basic modal i-VII-i progression, Am and G. These examples will sound generically modal. The only difference between A aeolian and A dorian, as we shall see below, is that aeolian has a minor sixth scale degree, F, while dorian has a major sixth scale degree, F♯. The minor pentatonic has neither, and neither do these examples.

A Aeolian

Aeolian is the modal name for what is also called the pure minor or natural minor scale. It is the relative minor scale to the major scale a minor sixth below it (i.e. A minor and C major are relative minor and major scales, sharing the same key signature). We will first look at the scale in its fiddle tune modal context.

The scale is spelled A, B, C, D, E, F, G.   Here are a few repertoire excerpts:

Here is the A aeolian scale and a few runs. As always, memorize the scale and play around with it on your own.

We will use one final aeolian tune to illustrate a couple of points. Play the opening four measures of *Paddy Ryan's Dream*.

Paddy Ryan's Dream

What mode is that in? I have told you the difference between aeolian and dorian is the 6th scale degree, F in A aeolian, F♯ in A dorian. There is neither in our example. The 6th scale degree is the least used scale degree in the minor modes, often omitted for whole sections; or sometimes there is just one or two in the whole tune.

Also, note the G♯ in the fourth measure. Enslaved by modern harmonic rules, I called it an E7 chord, where it is really just a little melodic gesture. Anyway, you will see a mixture of modal and modern cadences in these tunes, just as mixolydian tunes sometimes have the modern V7-I cadence, in addition to the modal VII-I. We will discuss the V7-i cadence later.

Now play the second section of *Paddy Ryan's Dream*.

Here the aeolian modality asserts itself, with the F♮s in the second and next to last measures of this section. Don't be confused by the decorative F♯s in the first and fifth measures.

Aeolian Chord Progressions

Remember, some would say no accompaniment is best, or that the accompaniment should be simple drones of maybe diads, 1 and 5 with no 3rd. If using chords however, the most important are i, iv, v, and VII, with the basic cadence progression VII-i or v-i. In aeolian, or pure minor, the naturally occurring chords are minor chords on i, iv, and v; and major chords on III, VI, and VII (we omit ii-dim). In A aeolian, that means the naturally occurring chords are Am, Dm, Em; and C, F, G. You will see all of those chords either indicated by the editor, or suggested by the music.

Remember that in modal tunes, reasonable minds may differ on the harmonic analysis (or modern harmonic analysis doesn't work). For example, in A aeolian, Em and G, v and VII, can often fill the same place and may be equally suggested by the music. Some editors may suggest Em7, which has all the notes of both chords. Remember, the composer wasn't thinking of chord changes. As a single line player, you will just play melodically.

A Dorian

A dorian is spelled A, B, C, D, E, F#, G, so it is just the same as A aeolian, but with a major sixth degree, F# (nine half steps), compared with A aeolian, with its minor sixth scale degree, F♮, (eight half steps). The dorian formula is 1, 2, ♭3, 4, 5, 6, ♭7. There are more dorian tunes than aeolian.

Here are a few A dorian excerpts, notated with one sharp. You will also see dorian tunes notated in aeolian, with accidentals sharping the 6th scale degree.

The Old Grey Gander

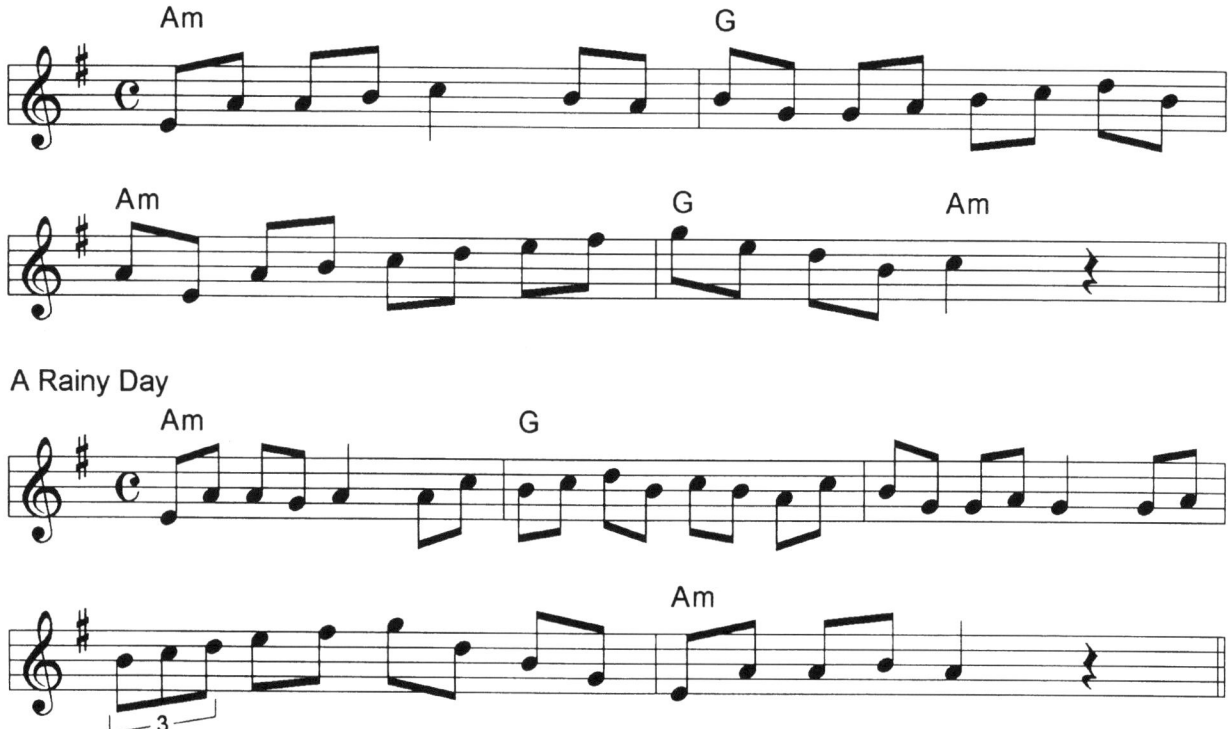

A Rainy Day

Note that in each of the last two excerpts, there is only one 6th scale degree, F#. The 6th scale degree is the least used note in the dorian mode, and it seems to me that when it occurs, it is most often ascending, or serving to decorate the 7th scale degree, G in A aeolian. See what you think. This observation is similar to the one I made during our major scale studies: that the 4th scale degree is the least used scale degree over the I chord in the major scale. And equally helpful.

More dorian runs:

A Rainy Day-second section

A few more dorian runs:

Dorian Chord Progressions

Traditionalists would say that like aeolian, the dorian mode is ill served by modern harmonic accompaniment and analysis. If used, the naturally occurring chords in the dorian mode are i, ii, III, IV, v, vi-dim (we omit), VII. In A dorian that means Am, Bm, C, D, Em, G. You will most often see Am, Em and G; i, v, and VII, but you may encounter any of the others. Noteworthy is that in dorian, you get a major chord on IV, instead of the minor iv of the aeolian mode.

I have room for this here: Nowadays, most people think of dorian as the second mode of the major scale; that is, using the notes of the major scale, with the second scale degree as the tonic. But it was not always so. By about 800 CE, Western music had settled on the seven notes which are the white keys on the piano, properly called the diatonic scale. But the first mode was dorian. The major scale was not allowed for church music until the 16th century, although it was popular for secular music, and referred to as *modus vulgaris*. So there. Go modes!

Modern Minor - V7-i

When playing a minor section or tune in folk or modern popular styles, you can just play aeolian or minor pentatonic over that section or tune, except perhaps for the cadences. Desirous of the advantages of the V7 chord: root movement down a fifth; the leading tone; and the tritone demanding resolution, modern minor cadences are usually V7-i cadences rather than the modal VII-i or v-i.

To get the V7 chord, it is necessary to alter the aeolian scale by raising the 7th scale degree one half step. In A minor, that means raising G to G♯. Play these two examples:

You can hear how the E7 run has more pull to the tonic, A. Here are a few more examples of the V7-i progression in A minor:

If you play traditional fiddle, or country or folk, it is probably just easiest to think of this as a little alteration of the minor scale. It has a name, however:

Harmonic Minor

The minor scale, altered to have a major seventh scale degree, is called the harmonic minor scale. It is used in classical music, and harmonic minor, technically, is what you are playing when you play V7-i. In classical music, when you learn the minor scale, you learn harmonic minor, and melodic minor (below), rather than aeolian.

As a scale, harmonic minor has an interesting and characteristic interval: the augmented second between the minor sixth scale degree, and the major seventh scale degree, F and G♯ in the following:

It is not a traditional sound, but you may find harmonic minor works very nicely in folk or folk rock, over i, iv, and of course V7, but not over v or VII. It makes a nice alternative to the tired old minor pentatonic that most other people will be playing. And if you want to be a gothic rock violinist, this is definitely the scale for you.

Jazz View - V7♭9♭13

As I said, if you just play traditional music, you can think of V7-i as requiring a little alteration of the minor scale to produce a major 7th scale degree. That gives you V7, and you play the scale, emphasizing chord tones of the V7 chord. If, however, you were to analyze the resulting scale from the fifth scale degree, root of the V7 chord, you would find that you are playing a dominant scale, but with a ♭9 (♭2nd) scale degree and ♭13 (♭6th) scale degree. If you learn it like that, you can use it in major keys as well, as a nifty altered dominant scale.

Adding the ♯9, F♯♯, to the scale would also be cool, giving you the E7♭9♯9♭13 scale.

Modern Dorian - ii7-V7-I

While there may not have been any recent Top Forty hits written in the dorian mode (since rock artist Carlos Santana in the 70's), it is still alive and well in contemporary Celtic music, heavy metal rock, and modal jazz. A touch of dorian over the i chord works nicely in many styles of folk or folk/rock, sounding a little jazz/rock, but not too far out. Dorian is also the scale of choice to play over ii7 in the fundamental jazz progression ii7-V7-I. We now turn our attention to that progression.

In traditional music, the fundamental major scale progression is V7-I. In jazz, it is ii7-V7-I. The ii7 chord can be viewed as simply substituting for the first part of V7, as they have two notes in common. (Substituting, for one chord, a different chord with overlapping notes is one of the basic elements of jazz harmony.) Every jazz method book has a chapter on the ii7-V7-I progression, and there are entire books on the subject.

First, about the ii7 chord. ii7 is a minor triad, with a ♭7 (minor 7th; 10 half steps). The naturally occurring 7th above all three minor triads in the major scale, ii, iii, and vi, are ♭7's. So the formula for the minor seventh chord is 1, ♭3, 5, ♭7. For Am7, that means A, C, E, G. Am7 is the ii7 chord in the key of G. We will look first at the Am7 arpeggio, then a few examples with the A dorian scale, sometimes called in this context the minor seventh scale, over ii7 in the key of G.

Melodic Minor

The melodic minor scale has two forms: Ascending, the lower part of the scale is aeolian; the upper part of the scale is the same as the major scale. The ascending formula is 1, 2, ♭3, 4, 5, 6, 7. Descending, it is the same as aeolian. We'll look at it in Am, but not in other minor keys.

The scale is usually encountered in classical music, although it is also used in jazz, with the ascending form used both going up and down, referred to as jazz minor.

iii Chord - Phrygian

Just for informational purposes, I will mention phrygian. Phrygian is like the aeolian mode, but with a ♭2 scale degree, B♭ in A phrygian. That is what you play over the iii chord of the major scale, when you play the notes of the major scale. For example, Am is the iii chord in the key of F major. If you play the notes of the F scale over the Am chord, you are playing phrygian as to that Am chord.

This ♭2 phrygian sound is not exploited much, but it is there. When you are just playing melodically with the parent major scale it is not noticeable. The phrygian scale is also used in flamenco, and so you would-be World Beat players need to work on it as a parent scale itself, especially starting on E. We will not look at it in the other minor keys. Here is one A phrygian example, notated properly, with one flat.

Anytime you hear the tag *phrygian* in connection with a scale, it means it has a ♭2nd scale degree; i.e., phrygian dominant, or phrygian major.

E Minor

We will start with the E minor triad: E, G, B.

Then we will look at the E minor pentatonic scale: E, G, A, B, D.

Then we will look at the E aeolian scale: E, F♯, G, A, B, C, D, and the E dorian scale: E, F♯, G, A, B, C♯, D.

Finally, we will look at modern uses of E minor sounds.

E Minor Triad

E minor is the relative minor of G major; they share the same set of notes, so their key signatures are the same. The E minor triad, E, G, B:

The finger pattern in the first measure is the same as I pointed out in A minor, but starting on the D string. Here is a basic i-VII-i modal chord progression, Em and D, using the Em triad:

90

Now we take our Em triad out of the key of Em, and put in other keys. We start with the key of D major, where Em functions as ii, in this I-ii-V7-I progression:

In the key of G major, Em functions as the vi chord in this I-vi-IV-V7-I progression. The second half of the example changes to I-vi-ii-V7-I, using Am to replace C.

And last, a few measures of Em functioning as iii in the key of C major:

E Minor Pentatonic

The E minor pentatonic scale is spelled E, G, A, B, D, which is the same set of notes as its relative major pentatonic, G.

Here is our basic modal i-VII-i progression, using the E minor pentatonic scale. Again, the minor pentatonic scale has no 6th scale degree (C or C♯), so these examples are neither aeolian nor dorian.

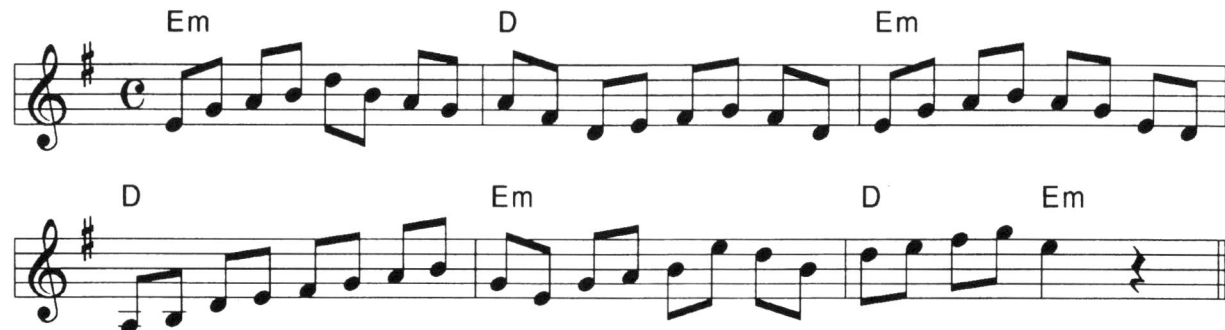

E Aeolian

E Aeolian is spelled E, F♯, G, A, B, C, D. It is the relative minor of G major; they share the same key signature. The basic aeolian progression, i-VII-i, is Em-D-Em. Here are a few repertoire excerpts:

Man of the House

E aeolian scale and runs:

Emote on your own.

Here are just a couple of more examples of aeolian sections with no 6th scale degree:

As you recall, aeolian has naturally occurring minor chords on i, iv, and v; and major chords on III, VI, and VII, (plus ii-dim). In E minor, that means Em, Am, and Bm; and G, C, and D.

E Dorian

E dorian is spelled E, F♯, G, A, B, C♯, D, so it is like E aeolian, but with C♯ rather than E aeolian's C♮. E dorian is properly notated with two sharps, but you will also see it notated with one sharp, as E aeolian, with the C's sharped as accidentals. Here are a few excerpts:

In dorian, the naturally occurring chords are minor chords on i, ii, and v; and major chords on III, IV, and VII, plus vi-dimin. In E dorian, that means Em, F#m, and Bm; and G, A, and D.

Modern Minor - V7-i

The V7-i cadence in E minor is B7-Em. To produce the B7 chord, it is necessary to raise D♮ to D#, the 3rd of the B7 chord.

Modern Dorian - ii7-V7-I

E dorian is the scale of choice when Em7 functions as ii7 in the key of D major. The Em7 chord is spelled E, G, B, D. We start with the Em7 arpeggio, and then look at a few ii7-V7-I's:

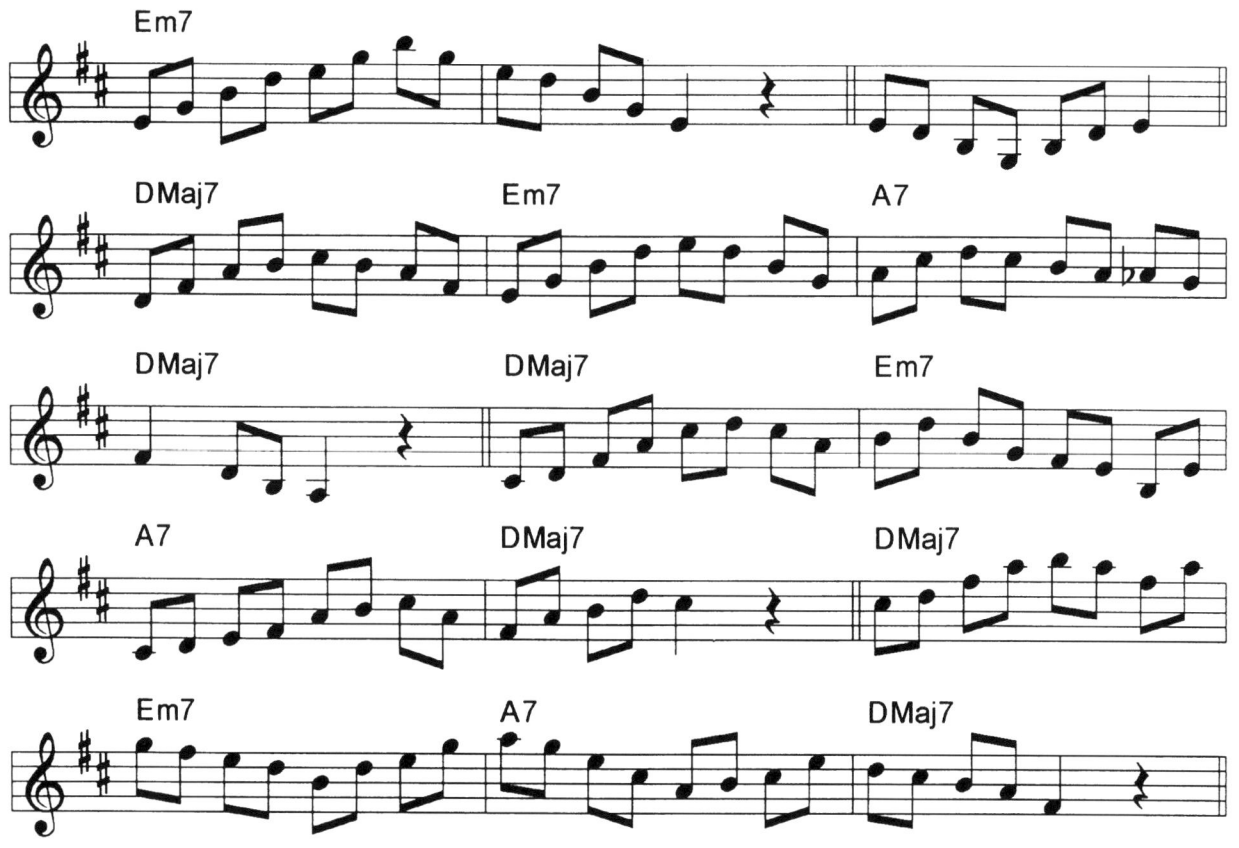

D Minor

The core dorian and aeolian fiddle keys are based on E and A. There are a few D aeolian and dorian tunes, but I include D minor because of its importance in other styles.

We will start with the D minor triad: D, F, A.

Then we will look at the D minor pentatonic scale: D, F, G, A, C.

Then we will look at the the D aeolian scale: D, E, F, G, A, B♭, C,
and the D dorian scale: D, E, F, G, A, B, C.

Finally, we look at modern sounds.

D Minor Triad

Here is our basic modal progression, i-VII-i, using the D minor triad and C major triad. D minor is the relative minor of F major, and shares the same key signature.

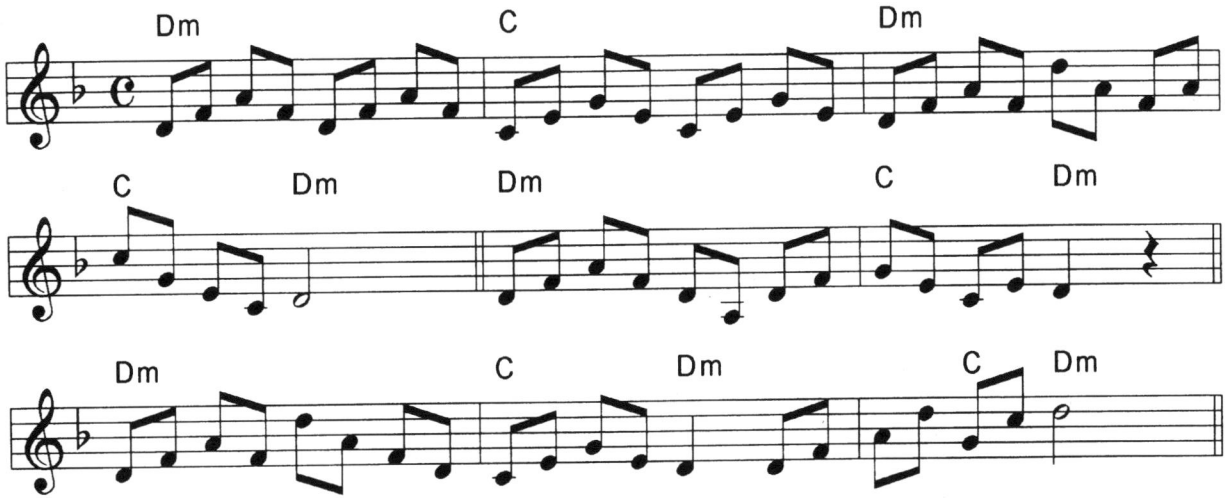

In the key of C major, Dm functions as the ii chord. Here are some C major chord progressions using the D minor triad:

In the key of F major, Dm functions as the vi chord:

Dm functions as iii in the key of B♭ major, but that is too far afield for us.

D Minor Pentatonic

The D minor pentatonic scale is spelled D, F, G, A, C. Note the little pattern on the middle strings when you play the scale.

Here is the D minor pentatonic scale in our basic modal progression, i-VII-i:

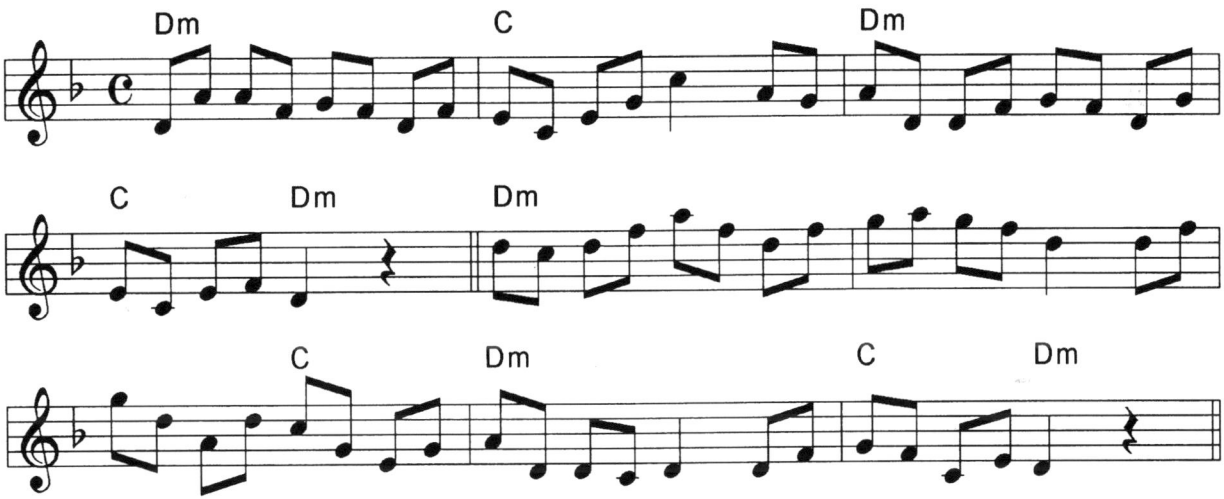

D Aeolian

D aeolian is spelled D, E, F, G, A, B♭, C. It is the relative minor of F major. Here it is, without repertoire excerpts:

D Dorian

D dorian is spelled D, E, F, G, A, B, C. Its relative major is C.

102

Modern D Minor - V7-i

In D minor, the V7 is A7. To produce A7, we change C to C#:

Modern D Dorian - ii7-V7-i

D dorian is the scale of choice to play over Dm7 functioning as ii7 in the key of C. First, the Dm7 arpeggio, D, F, A, C:

Now a few measures of I-ii7-V7-I:

Diminished

Diminished chords have a dissonant, unstable sound. Diminished chords are found in almost all styles of music. In old time fiddle music, diminished chords are used in rags, invariably in the progression IV-IV♯°-I (° is the symbol for diminished).

A word about terminology. We are referring to what are properly called fully diminished chords, with a formula of 1-♭3-♭5-♭♭7. The term *diminished* refers to the diminished 5th (♭5) in the chord. There is also a half-diminished chord, spelled 1-♭3-♭5-♭7. The half-diminished chord is commonly called a minor seventh ♭5th chord, for easily distinguishable terminology. It is often used in jazz, in minor keys, the progression going ii7♭5-V7-i. We will not discuss it further.

The diminished chord is spelled 1-♭3-♭5-♭♭7. This formula means the chord is made up of stacked minor thirds. The structure results in two interesting characteristics. First, you cannot go higher than the 7th. Above that, the notes start repeating, so there are no 9ths, 11ths, or 13ths. Second, it means that there are only three diminished chords in all of musicdom. If you build diminished chords on any three consecutive half steps, you will have used all twelve notes. There may be different spellings, i.e., C♯ = D♭, and any of the four notes of the chord can be considered the root, so the chord may have a different name depending on how it is stacked up, but there are only three different sets of actual pitches. So if you learn three fingerings, you have the whole deal covered.

IV-IV♯°-I

Again, in fiddle tunes, the diminished chord appears in rags, in the progression IV-IV♯°-I. In this context it is very easy to learn. We will look at the IV♯° chord in each of our main fiddle keys.

D Major - G♯°

Let's start with the key of D. The IV chord is G, and the IV♯° is G♯°. Play the following example:

That wasn't so tricky, was it? In fact, except for the G♯, it kind of had a familiar ring, didn't it? You are all thinking, "Yes, that G♯° was just like a G7 chord, but with G♯ instead of G." That is exactly right. IV♯° = IV7, with 4 changed to 4♯.

105

Here is a G Dominant run over the G chord, followed by the G#° arpeggio. The only difference is G changing to G#. By now, you can play dominant seventh arpeggios in your sleep (you can, can't you?). So this common rag progression should give you no problem at all. Remember, we are in the key of D, picking up the progression on the IV chord, G.

Of course, you do not have to lead into the diminished chord with IV7. I just used IV7 so you would only have to change one note. Here is the same progression, IV-IV#°-I, using a G major run leading to the IV#°:

Diminished Scale

The diminished arpeggio is sure neat and all, but what if you want to add some notes to make more melodic runs? There are two diminished scales. The more common is formed as follows: to each note of the diminished chord, add the note a half step below. It is almost easier to figure that out on the instrument than read it, but here is one example. Note that this yields an eight note scale, rather than the seven notes of the major, minor, dominant, and modal scales.

(The other, less used diminished scale adds the notes a half step above each chord tone.)

G Major - C#°

In G major, C is the IV chord, and C#° is the IV#°. Here is an example to put the chord in context. I am using a C7 arpeggio over the C chord, so the only note to change going to the diminished chord is C changing to C#.

Now a few more examples of C7 run leading to the C#, and back to the I chord, G:

And a few leading to the C#° from a C major run:

Here is one example of the C#° scale, adding to each chord tone the note one half step below it:

C Major - F#°

In the key of C major, the IV chord is F, and the IV#° chord is F#°. We use a F7 run to lead into F#°.

A few more measures, picking it up on the IV chord:

One example of the F♯° scale:

A Major - D♯°

In the key of A major, D is the IV chord, and D♯° is the IV♯°.

And again, picking it up on the IV chord, D:

Two comments: One, I have not expressly spelled the three diminished chords and asked you to memorize the notes. Instead, for our fiddle tune context, we are just learning them in relation to the IV chord, because that is how we find them. Two, note however, that this last one, D♯°, is the same as F♯°, the IV♯° for the key of C. D♯° is spelled D♯, F♯, A, C; and F♯° is spelled F♯, A, C, E♭, which are the same notes, stacked differently, and D♯ spelled as E♭ in F♯°. There are only three diminished chords, right?

Now one example of the D♯° scale, adding to each chord tone the note a half step below:

Note the diminished chord makes the following pattern on the fingerboard. In practice, it may be broken up with open strings, but it may help you get oriented if you start to get lost while playing.

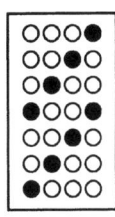

IV♯° = IV7♭9 (no root)

There is another way to look at the IV♯° chord. If you take, for example, G♯°, (G♯, B, D, F), and view the G♯ as A♭, you could analyze it as being a G7♭9 chord, (G, B, D, F, A♭), but without the G being played. This would be viewing the chord simply as an altered dominant. If you can play the IV dominant scale over the IV chord, then you can (in theory) play altered dominant runs also. The 7♭9 is the most basic altered dominant. Just change the major 9th, A, to ♭9, A♭, and otherwise play the IV dominant scale. An example follows. It is almost the same as the diminished scale.

Passing Diminished Chords

Here is a common jazz progression, using I♯° and II♯°. The use is similar to the IV♯° we have looked at, but it merits a separate look.

this might be better expressed as G7♭9

Decorative Diminished Chords

Diminished chords can also decorate a chord of long duration, by using the diminished chord of the same root, then returning to the original chord.

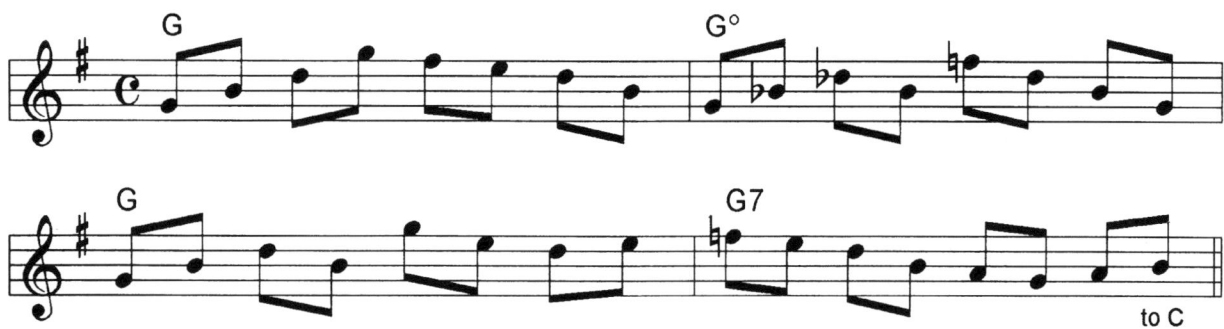

to C

Blues

While blues is certainly out of place in American/Celtic traditional fiddling, blues, blues based playing, and use of the blue notes, ♭3, ♭7, and ♭5, has become a very important part of popular music, including jazz/swing, country and rock.

Form

The most common blues progression is the 12-bar blues:

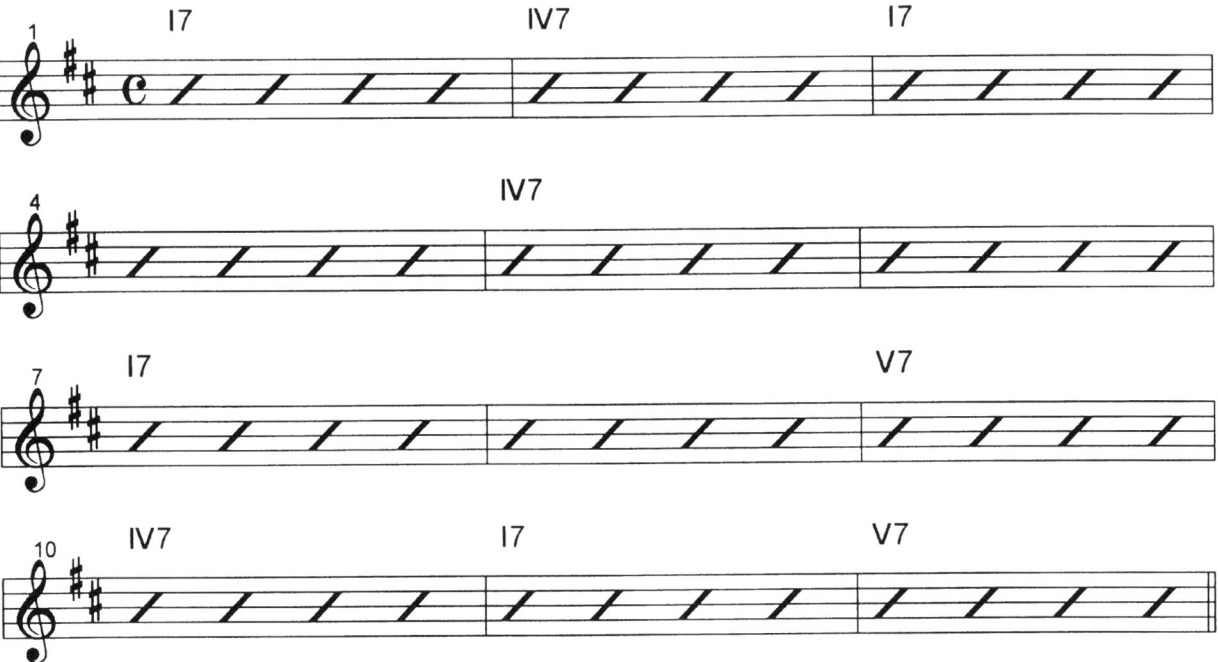

Note that the progression uses the three major chords of the major scale, I, IV and V. All the chords are played as dominant chords, favored for the jangly color. Country blues may use plain old 7th chords, while more sophisticated blues may use higher extensions of the chords, 9ths and 13ths. Jazz players may use altered dominant chords.

The above example is the 12-bar blues, the most common. There are variations. The most common include playing I7 instead of IV7 in the second measure, and making a 16 bar form by increasing chord durations. Jazz blues may have other chord substitutions, such as a cycle of fifths in measures seven through ten, or as a turnaround at the end.

Blues Scale

The blues scale is spelled 1, b3, 4, b5, 5, b7, so it is the same as the minor pentatonic scale, with the addition of b5, the bluest of the blue notes. Often, the minor pentatonic scale is used, rather than the whole blues scale, more in rock than other styles. So the blues is a minor type scale, played over major based chords (there are some minor chord blues, also).

Blues in D

Here is the D blues scale, D, F, G, Ab, A, C. We are notating these examples in D major, which is correct, but sure takes a lot of accidentals. You need to play all of the blues examples in swing rhythm, approximately:

Here is a standard, 12-bar blues progression, using the D blues scale:

Try that on your own, and try some measures of D minor pentatonic to hear the slightly different sound. Notice how the minor pentatonic makes that boxy pattern on the two middle strings. It's easy, and true hokum, to run up and down the minor pentatonic scale at a million miles an hour. Or do your endless scale pattern with minor pentatonic.

Blues Ostinati

Here are three blues bass patterns, which have been adopted by guitar and horn players. They can be played behind the singer or when someone else is soloing. I include them because everybody ought to know them. I have not written out a whole blues progression; I have just written the pattern for each of the three chords. The second pattern can be thought of as using the dominant scale built on each chord root, and the third pattern is its pentatonic or 6th chord cousin.

Blues in G

The G blues scale is spelled G, B♭, C, D♭, D, F.

Before we play 12 bars of G blues, let's revisit an element introduced on p. 62:

This example features a common blues figure, the ♭3rd scale degree ascending to the major 3rd, B♭ up to B in our example. You can slide up from ♭3 to 3, or you can slur it, or you can trill it, or anything else you can think of. What is being sought is the *blue third*. It is often expressed or implied by using ♭3 in addition to or instead of 3 in the dominant scale, or indeed in the major scale; or in something like the figure above. The real blue third lies somewhere between 3 and ♭3, maybe a little closer to ♭3. On the fiddle, you can, of course, intonate the 3rd anywhere you want.

Here is our standard 12 bar blues in G:

Here are the same ostinato patterns we looked at in D:

A chromatic walking bass pattern:

What else can you play?

In straight up blues playing, the most common thing to do is to play the blues scale or the minor pentatonic scale over the whole progression. But other scales are used also. Here are the most common scales used in blues playing:

1. The blues scale, or minor pentatonic, over the whole progression.

2. I dominant, IV dominant, and V dominant. This is the swing and jazz way to play blues, and it used to be the country way to play blues, although minor pentatonic rock based playing is now current in Nashville (remember: Rock didn't ruin Country; People ruined Country). Mixed in especially on I, is the ♭3. In jazz, alterations, or bop dominant, putting the major 7th scale degree as a passing tone between 1 and ♭7; it keeps the dominant seventh chord tones falling every other note, so it is easy to keep them all on the beat. It doesn't sound all that jazzy; try it.

3. Add the 6th scale degree, and 2nd (9th) scale degree to the blues scale, which is about like #2.

4. I, IV, and V major pentatonic. A little touch can brighten things up.

Let's look at some of those while learning the A blues scale.

Blues in A

The A blues scale is spelled A, C, D, E♭, E, G. Since it will take you about a second and a half to learn the scale, we will mix in some of the above alternate scales in the following progression:

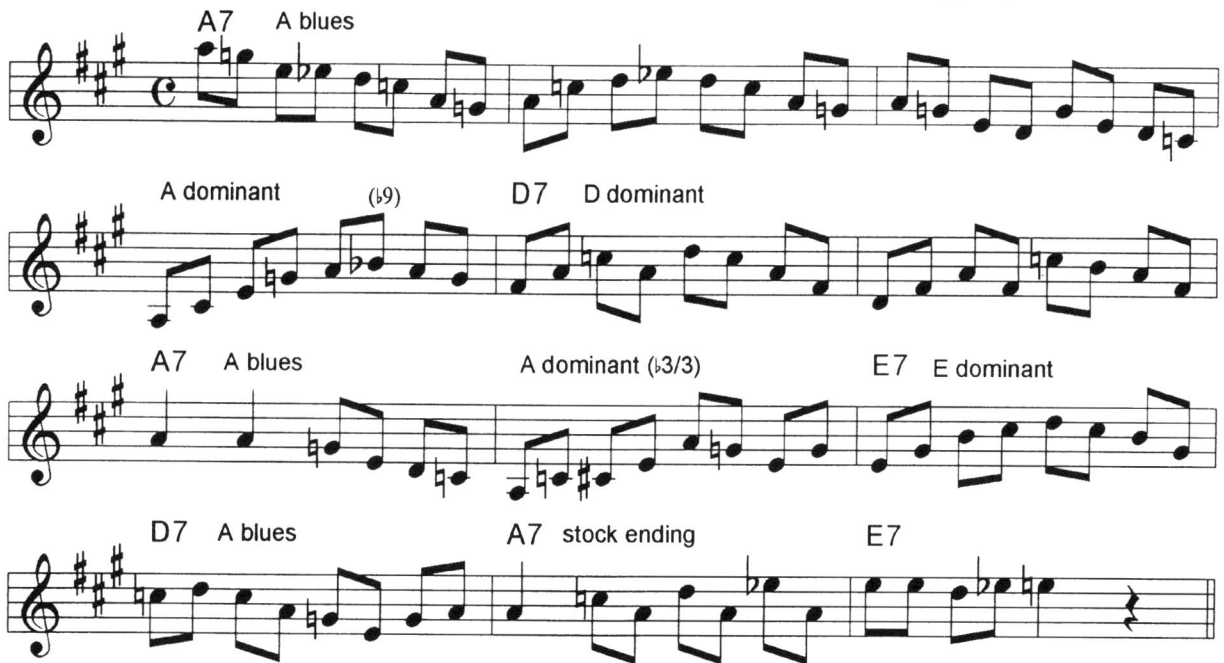

Blues in C

The C blues scale is spelled C, E♭, F, G♭, G, B♭. Play that a few times. Note there are no open strings in the basic C blues scale, except the G string. Note the patterns. The following twelve bars uses the C blues scale in the first measure, and we then continue to look at alternate scales. This is a much more swing blues, as you will see.

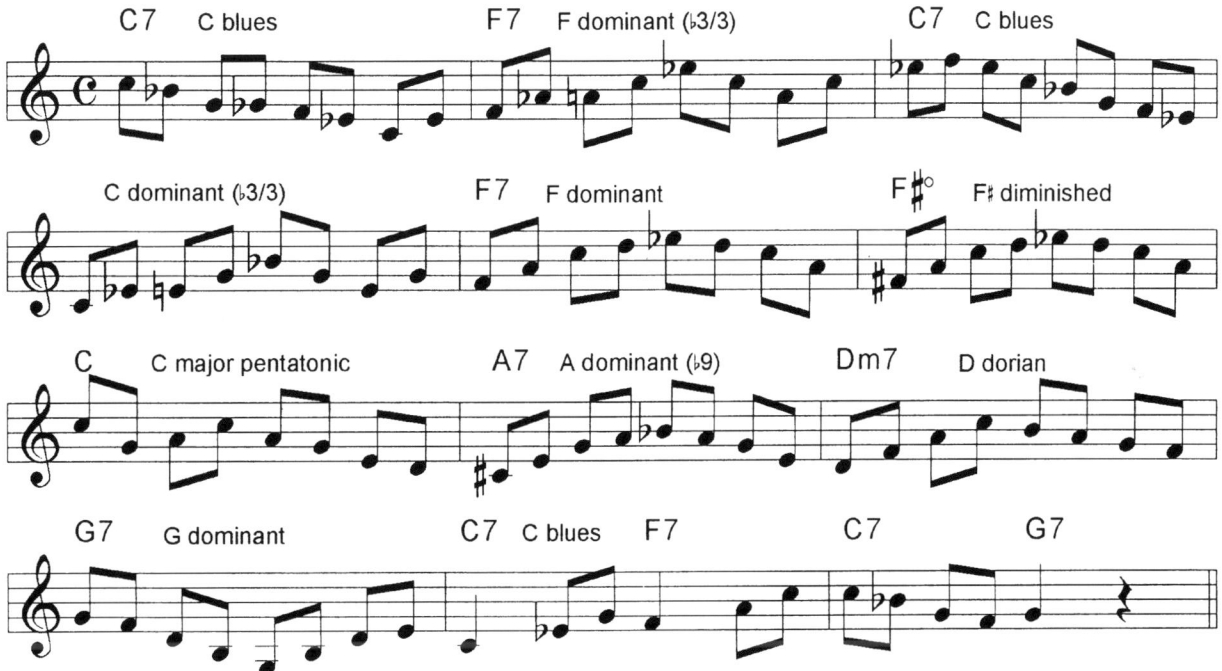

Blues in E

We have done our core keys, but blues in E is so common, I can't leave it out. The blues scale is spelled E, G, A, B♭, B, D. We won't do a whole progression, but here is the scale:

A Modest Essay

One of the appealing things about fiddle music is its antiquity. While researching (read: blundering about), I found some things which didn't fit in anywhere, or would complicate the text too much. What follows is not real scholarship, but a summary of what I think I have found, to give you some background for when you read about this stuff elsewhere.

Is there a natural basis to our scales and harmony? I believe the answer is yes, with some questions as to how far you can take it. There is absolutely a naturally favored relationship between a note and the note a perfect fifth above it. Its nearly universal recognition in human music as a special relationship strongly indicates humans have some predisposition to like the perfect fifth. It is pleasing to our ears, and is the most stable sounding harmonic interval except the octave. The human ear may find it easier to deal with the comparatively uncomplicated vibrations caused by intervals with simple ratios, such as the 1:2 of the octave, and 2:3 of the perfect fifth. Further, the perfect fifth is the second overtone, after the octave. For those of you who don't know this: when a string or column of air vibrates fast enough for us to hear it as a tone, it vibrates not only at the frequency which produces the fundamental tone, but also at other higher frequencies, called overtones. We hear the first six or eight of these overtones, and it is their relative strength that gives individual instruments their timbre; that is, a fiddle sounds like a fiddle and pipes sound like pipes. The perfect fourth is the inverse of the perfect fifth, and it too has been widely regarded as special, although it is not nearly as stable sounding. Laboratory experiments bear all this out.

Although you can find plenty of exceptions, humans seem to favor discreet intervals approximately like whole steps, rather than very close intervals. Likely this is modeled after the melodic steps of human speech (the range of most music is similarly within the general range of the human voice). With the octave divided by the fourth and fifth, filling in with whole steps or larger intervals could easily yield the pentatonic scale, with its intervals of whole steps and minor thirds. The theory might then continue: put a half step in each of the minor thirds, and *voila!,* the major scale and other modes. Let's look further.

Pentatonic scales: If you look in music textbooks, the pentatonic scale is spelled: 1, 2, 4, 5, 6 of the major scale, the so called Chinese pentatonic scale. This is not the same formula as either the major or minor pentatonic scales we studied; the major pentatonic scale would be the segment from 4 to 4 an octave above, and the minor pentatonic would start on 2. Some musicologists say there is only one parent pentatonic scale and the others are its modes; others say there are different pentatonic scales. One interesting thing about the 12456 scale that it does not have either a third or a seventh, which are the intervals most important to giving our major and modal scales their characters.

Anyway, these various pentatonic scales, properly called nonhemitonic (no half steps) pentatonic scales are nearly universal, and are found in all European folk music, indicating some natural or acoustic forces incline us to them.

The diatonic scale is the proper name for the octave divided into seven intervals as on the white keys of the piano, but without assigning any particular note as the starting point. Therefore the major scale is but one mode of the diatonic scale, as are dorian, etc. The earliest Western music preserved in notation is plainchant, from the tenth century, at which time the diatonic scale was firmly established, and had been for hundreds of years. We know the source for early Christian chant was Jewish psalmody. Does that mean we got it from Jewish psalmody, or is it older and more universal? Recently, archeologists found a piece of a Neanderthal flute, made from the femur of a cave bear, dated between 43,000 and 82,000 years old. Based on the unequal spacing of the holes, and some other reasonable reconstructive assumptions, there is a good case made that the flute would have played a segment of the diatonic scale, specifically a minor mode segment. Similarly, the oldest transcribed musical fragment, a 4,000 year old song from Ur, appears to be a segment of the diatonic scale. Some African and near Eastern cultures have diatonic music which has developed independently of the West, although it is not as widespread as the pentatonic scale, and there are many musical systems that are not remotely like it. All this may indicate some natural human predisposition towards the diatonic scale.

As to whether the diatonic scale is a filled-in pentatonic scale, the evidence is unclear, but certainly the pentatonic scale is found many places where the diatonic is not. It may be that they are independent but equal, both with some acoustic or natural basis, and both very, very, old.

Are the fiddle modes the same as the church modes? No and maybe. There was more to the Church modes than the scale built upon a given root, called the *finalis*. There also was range, called *ambitus,* and the dominant of the authentic modes was a fifth above the *finalis,* but a third above the *finalis* in the plagal modes (the term dominant is sometimes used in a broad sense meaning whatever note after the tonic is the secondary tonal center; in modes it is sometimes called cotonic).

Those differences beg the question however, of whether the source of those scales in fiddle music is the Church modes, or an independent folk origin. The evidence suggests that an independent and parallel folk origin may be there, and that the Church mode names may be best viewed as a convenient classification system. (Scholars now refer to the modes by number, rather than by name.) The amount of cross influence between church and secular music in the early years is unknowable.

In his book *Traditional Music in Ireland* (Ossian), Thomas Ó Canainn asserts mode is not enough to comprehend modal tunes, and that one must look to such factors as note frequency, placement, and duration to determine the true tonic and dominant, using those terms in the broad sense.

How old are the tunes themselves? We don't know. The earliest transcriptions of Irish music are from the early 18th century, and represent tunes many years old, perhaps centuries. Included are tunes still being played today, in some form. The jig became popular in the 16th century. So 16th century is about the earliest you can speculate without being too Romantic. There must be survivors of some truly ancient melodies, but no one can say which ones, and the passage of time and the influence of the changes in music has surely altered them. However, "modern prejudice tends to impose an arbitrary limit of three of four centuries upon folk memory, without argument or evidence; for the narrow experience of literate Europe is unacquainted with the long memory of illiterate societies, and easily condemns uncritically what it does not understand. In India the background setting of the early Hindu gods has persisted in oral tradition for something over 3,000 years; the furthest recollections of Irish legend claim no greater antiquity." (*The*

Age of Author, by John Morris [Phoenix], p. 150)

The major scale has been dominant since about 1650 or 1700 to 1900, the so called Common Practice Era. Modern music education teaches music history as an evolution from less sophisticated music and harmonic practices beginning with organum in the 10th century, and ending with the ultimate expressions of harmonic and tonal truth, the major triad and major scale. It has been observed that the modal system affords much more variety in melodic expression than the major/minor scale system, and that the atonality of the 20th century, the interest in new sounds, blue notes, and renewed interest in the other modes, shows the major scale is not the end-all of music. Still, however, most tunes, even among the oldest, are major scale. Some try to derive the major scale from the overtone series, pointing out that after octave, fifth, octave, comes the major third, thus generating the major triad. They try to take it too far however, in trying to generate the whole major scale that way. To do so, they "invert" the fifth to get the perfect fourth, because the first fourth in the overtone series is ♮4. Or they use the overtones of the overtones. However, even if those methods are suspect, the underlying physics are there, and the success of the major triad and scale may indicate some natural basis for our favoring the major sound.

Postscript

If you have worked your way through the book, I am immensely grateful for your perseverance, and I hope you learned some things that will be of value to you in your musical endeavors. I have three suggestions to make in closing.

First, while I am not a New Age kind of guy, I believe in visualization. If you can clearly see, in your mind's eye, a finger pattern, or a bowing pattern, you are more likely to be able to play it. This means you can, in effect, practice your instrument by daydreaming about it.

Second, to find your own voice on the instrument, try singing or humming phrases of your own, or just parts of phrases, and play them back on the instrument. Your voice is unencumbered by the ruts and technical limitations of your playing. Singing phrases will make you move your fingers in new ways, and it will really be your musical voice. This is especially true on the fiddle, which is more like the human voice in its expressions than any other instrument.

Third, forget everything you learned in the book, and play your musical thoughts, not scales and arpeggios. The eminent Edward Van Halen said, "To me, you got ... twelve notes, and you mix them up however you want. Whoever said if you play them in a certain order it's this scale, or if you play them in that order it's that scale?" (*Guitar Player*, March 1995)

Jazz guitar guru Ted Greene once took a lesson from the legendary Joe Pass, from whom music flowed like water. Joe was playing a line, and Ted stopped him and asked, "What are you thinking of?" Joe's reply, "Nuthin'." May you all get there.

Made in the USA
Middletown, DE
15 August 2018